It's all FREE for Seniors

John Clarke

It's All FREE for Seniors

John Clarke

Copyright © MMIII de Swartes Ltd, London

New edition published MMXI by The Windsor Group,
Hamilton House,
2 Station Road,
Epping
CM16 4HA

Copyright © MMXI The Windsor Group (This Edition)

Typeset by SJ Design and Publishing, Bromley, Kent

ISBN 978-1-903904-16-9

Contents

Notice to Readers

Whilst every effort has been made to ensure the accuracy of the information provided in this publication, neither the author nor the publisher can accept responsibility or liability for that information, this including any of the opinions or advice expressed in the following pages.

Introduction

To me, fair friend, you never can be old,
For as you were when first your eye I ey'd
Such seems your beauty still. Three winters cold
Have from the forests shook three summers pride,
Three beauteous springs to yellow autumn turn'd
In process of the seasons have I seen,
Three April perfumes in three hot Junes burn'd
Since first I saw you fresh, which yet are green
Ah! Yet doth beauty, like a dial-hand,
Steal from his figure, and no pace perceiv'd;
So your sweet hue, which methinks still doth stand,
Hath motion, and mine eye may be deceiv'd;
For fear of which, hear this, thou age unbread:
Ere you were born was beauty's summer dead
(William Shakespeare)

This book is just for YOU! The more mature . . . or if you prefer, the Senior Citizen. It has been written because there are many who have a basic pension of say £75.50 and less than £3,000 in savings. It has been written to give you an overview of what's available free and to make you feel a whole lot better about the Autumn and Winter of Life.

This is a book to read and find out what you are entitled to and to help you discover whether or not assistance is available, should you have a financial problem now or in the future. This book will also guide you to where you should make the initial enquiry and how to go about it. At the end of the book you will find useful selections of contact names and addresses which will be a source of even further information.

Chapter One

Low Income

A VARIETY OF BENEFITS

These are benefits that depend on your savings and income and are not founded on National Insurance contributions.

You may be able to get benefit to help with your living costs, your rent and your Council Tax. You may also be entitled to help with other costs like prescriptions. Obviously there are rules. For instance, if you are being taken care of in a home, things would be different.

If you are not being taken care of in a home and you have less than £6,000 savings you may be able to get help with weekly living costs.

If you are still working, the regulations are again different. There may or may not be help in this respect. It all depends on your work.

There are different benefits for people who work less than 16 hours a week and for people who work 16 hours or more.

If you work fewer than 16 hours a week and are no older than 59, you may be able to claim Income Support, or income-based Jobseeker's Allowance if you're below retirement age (currently 65 for men and 60 for women).

You will not be eligible for these benefits if you have more than £16,000 in savings or if you have a partner living with you who works 24 hours a week or more.

However, your partner may be able to claim Working Tax Credit instead. This applies whether or not you are married, in a civil partnership or just living together.

If you are not sure how the hours you work will be treated for benefit purposes, you should consult an experienced adviser – for example, at a Citizens' Advice Bureau.

You can get Pension Credit if you are 60 or over. It does not matter what age your partner is. You must be living in the UK and not have any immigration controls on your stay here that would stop you claiming benefits.

Your income must be below a certain amount. The amount depends on your circumstances. There is no limit on how much capital – that is savings and property – you can have, but you will be treated as having income from any of your capital above £6,000 (£10,000 if you live in a care home).

If you are under sixty and ill or a carer, you will not need to sign on as unemployed to receive this benefit.

You would have to make a claim for Pension Credit. You should claim Pension Credit on the form PC1, which is obtainable by telephone, or in person at a Pension Service surgery, benefit office or local authority housing benefit or council tax benefit office. The national telephone help line for Pension Credit is 0800 99 1234 (textphone 0800 169 0133).

NOTE: Capital means anything that could provide you with a source of income. It includes savings, property and land. However this does not include your personal possessions or your home.

Capital of more than £6,000 will affect how much Income Support you get. Regardless of how much money you actually receive from your capital – if any – you will be seen as getting £1 a week in income for every £250 of capital (or part of £250) above the £6,000 limit.

If you own your home, they sometimes include an amount for interest repayments on your mortgage, or on a loan, which you may have taken out in respect of repairs or home improvements.

HOUSING AND COUNCIL TAX BENEFIT

Housing Benefit is a benefit for those people who are on a low income. It is to help them pay their rent.

You may be able to get Housing Benefit if you are on other benefits, work part-time or work full-time on a low income. You cannot get Housing Benefit to help with the costs of a mortgage or home loan.

If you are an owner-occupier, you may be able to get help with your mortgage interest through Income Support, income-based Jobseeker's Allowance or Pension Credit. However, if you are already on Income Support, it is possible to receive help in the form of Housing Benefit and Council Tax. In both cases your savings would affect these benefits.

You will not be able to get any Council Tax Benefit if you have capital (savings or property) worth over £16,000. If you have capital over £6,000, you will be assumed to have some income from that capital, and this will reduce the amount of Council Tax Benefit you can get.

The type of help you receive depends solely on your income and that of your partner, plus your expenses on necessities. If your income and savings are too high to receive Income Support, it is still feasible, depending on your circumstances, to receive at least some Housing or Council Tax Benefit – maybe both.

A Second Adult Rebate is possible for someone over eighteen years, living with you, based on a low rate of income and not paying rent or Council Tax. All the aspects depend on quite a few factors, such as:

- ☐ If you live with someone else, other than your partner, who must be 18 or over, not paying rent, not responsible to pay Council Tax, and have income below a certain amount. The other person will be included when the local authority work out whether or not you can get a discount on the amount of Council Tax you pay.
- ☐ Your income and savings.
- ☐ How much rent and Council Tax you are already paying.
- ☐ Persons within the family.
- ☐ How old you are.
- ☐ If you are disabled.

You can claim Council Tax Benefit by telephone if your local authority has published a phone number for making telephone claims. You may be able to make a claim for Council Tax Benefit by email or on the Internet. It's up to your local authority to decide whether to allow electronic claims. Forms are obtainable at your local Library, Post Office or Social Security office. If you apply for Income Support, you will automatically receive a claim form for Housing and Council Tax Benefit.

Chapter Two

The Social Fund

Sometimes, when additional expenses have to be met, you may not have enough money to cover them and this may cause a great deal of concern. However, there is a special fund known as 'The Social Fund' to help out at such times. Sometimes payments can be made in the form of a lump sum to cover extra expenses. Your circumstances would be investigated carefully. An application form would have to be completed and the Social Fund Officer would give priority in respect of high priority requirements.

Once completed the application form should either be sent or returned to your local Social Security office. The address, if not on an envelope supplied with the application form, can be found in the telephone directory. If you have access to the Internet, then this is another way of find the address. Any person receiving Income Support, Family Credit, Disability Working Allowance, Housing Benefit or Council Tax Benefit may receive help by the following payments which come from the Social Fund.

COLD WEATHER PAYMENTS

Do not confuse this with Winter Fuel payments, which are made regularly, every winter, to help people over sixty years of age regardless of the temperature. Cold weather payments are to help people on a low income with fuel costs during periods of cold weather. However, it does not matter what the money is spent on and these payments do not have to be repaid.

Each area of the country is linked to a weather station. When the weather forecasts or records an average daily temperature of zero degrees centigrade or less for seven consecutive days an automatic payment is made. If you are entitled to cold weather payments, you will receive £8.50 for each period of cold weather automatically. You do not have to make a claim for a cold weather payment, but if you feel you should have received one and did not, then you can make a written claim to your local benefit office, or get in touch with your local Citizens' Advice Bureau.

FUNERAL PAYMENT

Depending on your income and circumstances, you may be able to claim certain benefits if you lived with or were dependent on the deceased. Time limits apply, so check the details as early as possible.

Check whether there are other benefits you can claim, or whether your current benefits need to change.

The help you receive, in the above circumstances, depends on your personal savings and those of your partner (if applicable). These factors will be taken into consideration, as will the amount of money becoming available after the death. Although the Funeral Payment is not a loan, it may have to be repaid from the assets of the deceased.

The claim should be made on form SF200, available from your Jobcentre Plus office. In England, Wales and Scotland you can also apply by filling in an application form on-line on the Department for Work and Pensions website at *www.dwp.gov.uk*, although you will need to print the form in order to sign it. You have to have a funeral director's bill to apply for a funeral payment, and you will need to provide this with your claim.

There may also be a counselling scheme in respect of bereavement. If the deceased person passed away at a hospital, sometimes you can receive counselling there and will probably be asked if you wish to receive it. Otherwise it is possible to obtain further assistance or guidance by contacting the Social Services Office, Citizens' Advice Bureau or Registrar of Birth, Marriage and Deaths. There are leaflets available, one of which is entitled *What to do After a Death*.

(See also the section on Depression).

CRISIS LOANS

Crisis Loans have to be repaid. It is a loan used to help an individual or persons in the case of an emergency or a particular crisis in respect of a special need. Perhaps used for short-term expense, or in the case of a disaster, whereby the health and safety of the family or someone else is endangered.

The loan may be granted in respect of travel, living expenses or a household item. Income is taken into consideration although you do not have to be the recipient of Income Support or any other benefit. The loan is interest free; in other words you only have to pay back exactly the amount of money you borrowed.

The benefit office will tell you whether they can pay you anything, and if so how much. There is no minimum amount that can be awarded. Maximum amount is £1,500, but there are also set maximum amounts for living expenses. The maximum for other expenses is the reasonable cost of the item or service you need. When deciding how much to award, the benefit office will take into account how much you can afford to repay. Loans should normally be repaid within 104 weeks (2 years).

If you or your partner, (if you have one), have any savings or other money, this may affect how much money you receive.

Certain groups of people can only get a crisis loan in exceptional situations, for example students, those on strike and persons who may have been disallowed from other benefits. Immigration status will also affect whether you can get a crisis loan or not.

If you are uncertain as to whether or not you would be able to obtain a crisis loan, consult an experienced adviser, for example, at a Citizens' Advice Bureau. The form for this claim is SF401.

COMMUNITY CARE GRANTS

These are grants which go towards helping people to continue living independently at home. They also allow people to stay within a community or to become more independent within that community. Community Care Grants are used for many other reasons, for example, certain travel costs, removals, minor house repairs, blankets, furniture, cookers, beds, etc. You will find more information on the Community Care Grant on the following pages.

BUDGETING LOANS

A Budgeting Loan is allowed up to £1,500 maximum, £100 minimum. If you have been getting Income Support for at least twenty-six weeks, your application will be considered. This loan would be repayable over a period of time, but there would be no interest to pay. These loans are made in an effort to help you buy an item you may need but cannot afford. You might be able to obtain a Budgeting Loan to help with major equipment such as furniture. Repayment amounts depend on income and situation. A related payment would be a Crisis Loan.

You can apply on form SF500, which is available from local benefit offices. The form is also online on the Department for Work and Pensions website at *www.dwp.gov.uk*.

A loan should normally be repaid within 104 weeks (2 years).

APPLYING FOR SOCIAL FUND PAYMENTS

Except for the Cold Weather payments, the Social Fund payment depends on your savings.

- □ If your partner or yourself are under sixty years of age and have savings of over £1,000 this might affect how much money you could receive.
- □ If your partner or yourself are over sixty years of age and have savings of over £2,000, this might affect how much money you could receive.

To receive a payment from the Social Fund you will normally have to be receiving Income Support. However, to acquire a Crisis Loan you do not necessarily have to be receiving Income Support. Payment cannot be made if £1,500 or more is already owed to the Social Fund. People already receiving assistance with Housing Benefit and/or Council Tax Benefit will be able to receive help with funeral expenses. There are set rules in respect of both Cold Weather and Funeral Payments. Other

Social Fund payments are discretionary. Not everyone who applies will receive help from this particular fund.

Contact your local authority for an application form or obtain one from your local Library, Post Office, Social Security Office or on line.

DISCRETIONARY SOCIAL FUND

You may be eligible for a Community Care Grant if you are receiving:
- Income Support,
- Income-based Jobseeker's Allowance, or
- Pension Credit.
- You may also be eligible for a grant if in the next six weeks you are leaving institutional or residential care and you are likely to receive any of the above benefits.

You may be able to receive a Community Care Grant:
- If you are moving to a new home;
- Coming out of hospital to another home;
- Require help with removal expenses from your home to another with more suitable accommodation;
- Moving for any other reason.

You may also receive this grant to enable you to stay in your own home, so that you do not have to go into hospital or a care home.

If there are difficulties or problems within your family circle – maybe someone has become ill or disabled – you could receive help by applying for this grant.

If it is a necessity for you to travel, for example, to visit someone ill in hospital, you should be able to obtain help with this expense by applying for a Community Care Grant. Any Community Care Grant you can get will be reduced if you or your partner has capital/savings of more than £500 (£1,000 if one of you are aged 60 or over). If you have more capital than this, but not enough to pay for the item or service you need, you can apply for a grant to make up the difference. You can apply for a Community Care Grant on form SF300, available from local benefit offices. In England, Wales and Scotland, the form is also available online on the Department for Work and Pensions website at *www.dwp.gov.uk*, although you will need to print the form in order to sign it.

If you have the facility of a computer and access to the Internet at home or at your local library, a useful web address is:

http://www.carersuk.org/Information/Orderpublications/Factsheetsbooklets

This site has leaflets, fact sheets and booklets, which can be downloaded free of charge. For more information on Loans and Community Care Grants from the Social Fund, contact your local Social Security Office, the number of which is in your telephone directory or contact your local Citizens' Advice Bureau.

HOUSE REPAIRS

Obtaining a grant for certain repairs is possible when you want to adapt your home or carry out improvements. There would have to be an assessment of your income and savings. These grants are not available to council tenants or landlords.

If you are on Income Support, it may be possible for you to obtain a Community Care Grant or Budgeting Loan to help with minor repairs or redecorations. Obtaining additional Income Support to cover the interest on an independent loan may also be possible.

HOUSE RENOVATION GRANTS

The grant covers repairs, enhancements, insulation of roof space, heating systems, conversions and improvements to deficient inside living conditions, although there are certain requirements to be met.

It is available to:

☐ The more mature who cannot afford to have renovations carried out on their property;

☐ Those who are disabled and need to function within the home in a more independent way;

☐ Those owner/occupiers, landlords or tenants responsible for carrying out work on a leased property.

The financial circumstances of the person applying for the grant is important. The exception here is if the standard of the property has to be improved by bringing it in line with what is considered habitable.

Work would have to be approved by the council to ensure

requirements are appropriate to the state and age of the property.

- ☐ If you are an owner/occupier, this grant is mandatory.
- ☐ If you are the landlord, the grant is at the discretion of the Council.
- ☐ In all cases a means test is necessary.

Contact your local council authority for an application form. Information can be found at the library, Post Office and Citizens' Advice Bureau.

HOME ENERGY EFFICIENCY SCHEME (HEES)

The Home Energy Efficiency Scheme provides grants, which help to cover the costs of home insulation and of improving energy efficiency.

It is available to owner-occupiers and people renting accommodation. You may also be able to get other help with insulating your home.

GRANT UNDER HOME ENERGY EFFICIENCY SCHEME
The Warm Front Scheme (England)

Other schemes operate in Wales, Scotland and Northern Ireland.

In England you may be eligible for a Warm Front Grant. You may be eligible for a grant of up to £2,700 (or up to £4,000 if oil central heating is involved). You may receive a Warm Front Grant if you get one or more of the following:

- ☐ Income Support
- ☐ Housing Benefit
- ☐ Council Tax Benefit
- ☐ Income-based Jobseeker's Allowance
- ☐ Working Tax Credit
- ☐ Child Tax Credit
- ☐ Pension Credit
- ☐ Attendance Allowance
- ☐ Disability Living Allowance
- ☐ Industrial Injuries Disablement Benefit (which includes Constant Attendance Allowance)
- ☐ War Disablement Pension (which must include the mobility or Constant Attendance Allowance)

Even if you are not receiving any benefit, you may still be entitled to a Warm Front Grant. A check will be carried out to see if you are eligible for benefits and therefore a Warm Front Grant.

IMPROVEMENT AND/OR REPAIR GRANTS

You can apply for this if you are a landlord or landlord and tenant or tenant in a property that contains one or more apartments.

If you are the tenant applying for this grant, you must undertake the responsibility of contributing towards the work required. This particular grant can be obtained through your local council.

The Landlord's Main Responsibilities

There are certain repairs that will almost always be your landlord's responsibility, even if they are not specifically mentioned in the tenancy agreement. These are:

- The structure and exterior of the premises (such as walls, floors and window frames) and the drains, gutters and external pipes.
- If the property is a house, the essential means to access to it, such as steps from the street, are also included in 'structure and exterior'. Garden paths and steps are also included.
- Water and gas pipes and electrical wiring (including, for example, taps and sockets), basins, sinks, baths and toilets.
- Fixed heaters (for example, gas fires) and water heaters but not gas or electric cookers.

HOUSE IN MULTIPLE OCCUPATION

This grant has to be applied for by the landlord. The grant covers properties in which various people live – not properties in which the inhabitants are necessarily related or part of the same household.

The number of people living in a house of multiple occupation property will be taken into consideration when making the property fit for human habitation. This depends on certain aspects, for example whether there are sufficient washing and toilet facilities, fire and safety measures and cooking arrangements.

If you are successful in obtaining the grant, the standard of the property should be sufficiently raised to make it fit for human habitation.

COUNCIL AND HOUSING ASSOCIATION TENANTS

You have rights if you come under the above categories and these rights include your right to remain living in your home. It is the duty of the landlord to carry out repairs and you have the right to know if your rent can be increased or why it has been increased. If you need further details, please contact your local Citizens' Advice Bureau. If your home is privately rented and you need to know your rights, you will be able obtain information through Age Concern. Details at the rear of this book.

Under the *Landlord and Tenant Act 1985* for all tenancies which began after 24 October 1961, the landlord is responsible for all repairs to the structure, exterior and installations of the property. The only exception is if your tenancy was originally for a fixed term of more than seven years.

SECURITY IN THE HOME

Safety is important in the home. If you are a council tenant, the local authority may provide and fit security locks. If not, contact Help the Aged or your local Social Security Office. Issues worth considering are:
- Fire alarms.
- The front door (a 5-lever mortise lock for instance) and extra lighting.
- A safety chain.
- The back door and extra lighting.
- Security lights.
- An alarm system, linked to a telephone, so you could call for help.
- An entry phone.
- Windows secured with locks, which may be key operated.

SAFETY AT HOME – FIRE

The most important precaution you can take is to install smoke alarms in your home. Cutting down the risk of fire:
- Ensure you remove all pans from the stove after you have finished using them. Turn off the cooker. Never put tea towels on it.

- Never leave candles or cigarettes unattended.
- Ensure they are on a heat-resistant surface.
- Ensure they are extinguished before leaving the room.
- Keep kitchen appliances clean. Fat, oil, grease and crumbs build up and could catch fire.
- Plan your escape route, in case you need to use one in the event of fire. Keep your escape route clear and ensure everyone living in the house knows where the door and window keys are situated.
- If you have an open fire, ensure it is safe before leaving it unattended.
- All gas appliances and flues should be safety checked once a year.
- Landlords are responsible for arranging checks for rented accommodation.
- If you are a homeowner aged 60 or over, or disabled, you could, if so wish, join your supplier's Priority Service Register. This entitles you to a free annual check, among other benefits. Look on the back of your bill for details.
- Look out for scorched or hot plugs and sockets.
- Do not use equipment with frayed or taped leads.
- Do not use equipment with exposed wires.
- Turn off and unplug appliances when not in use unless they are designed to be left on (e.g. fridge, video recorder).
- Electric blankets should be tested every three years and replaced after 10 years.

CONTACT NAMES AND ADDRESSES FOR CRIME PREVENTION AND SAFETY IN THE HOUSE

British Safety Council
70 Chancellors Road, London W6 9RS

Victim Support National Centre
Hallam House, 56 - 60 Hallam Street, London W1W 6JL

National Security Inspectorate (Intruder Alarms)
Sentinel House, 5 Reform Road, Maidenhead SL6 8BY

Chapter Three

Freely Available Schemes

FREE AND INDEPENDENT PLANNING ADVICE

Planning Aid provides free, independent and professional help, advice and support on planning issues to people and communities who cannot afford to hire a planning consultant.

Planning Aid complements the work of local authorities but is wholly independent of them.

In most UK regions Planning Aid is run by the Royal Town Planning Institute (RTPI, a charity registered in England 262865 and Scotland SC 037841).

If you request help, a Planning Aid volunteer will get in touch with you to advise you. To contact either go to your public library, local Council Planning Department or get in touch with either your regional RTPI or if you cannot find it get in touch with:

The Royal Town Planning Institute
41 Botolph Lane, London EC3R 8DL
Telephone: 020 7929 9494: Fax: 020 7929 9490

TELEPHONE

Although there is no actual national scheme to provide help for seniors in respect of the telephone, certain people would receive assistance; that is if chronically sick or disabled.

If you are receiving Income Support you may be able to obtain a loan from the Social Fund. Sometimes it is possible to obtain help from certain local authorities and charities. BT has various schemes in respect of telephone usage. A call to Directory Enquiries should put you through to the correct department. If not, try the operator.

In certain circumstance it may be a good idea to consider a mobile phone. However, if you have little knowledge, or none at all, then please get advice from someone you know such as a friend, relative, social worker or carer.

TELEVISION LICENCES

A television licence is required for television receiving equipment (which includes television sets, video/DVD recorders, set-top boxes, TV-enabled PC etc) to receive and/or record television programme services, including terrestrial, digital, satellite or cable.

A licence is not required for equipment only used to replay prerecorded tapes/DVD.

A television licence covers you and anyone living at the premises as part of your family or as a guest, at the address stated on the licence.

There are television concessions:

- □ If you are 75 or over the TV licence is free.
- □ If you are registered blind.
- □ If you are retired or disabled and living in specific types of accommodation, such as residential care.

Although free, you do still need to have a licence. If your 75th birthday will fall in the year covered by the next licence, you can buy a short-term licence to cover you until your birthday, or you can claim a refund on an existing licence for the months since you reached the age of 75.

Once granted, the free over-75 licence is renewed automatically so you don't have to apply for a new one each year. If the over-75 licence holder dies, the TV licence continues to cover your household until it runs out.

If you are registered as blind, you will receive 50% off your television licence. For further information contact Age Concern or your Social Services Department.

CINEMAS AND THEATRES

Most cinemas and theatres provide concessions for people over pensionable age and for the unemployed or those on benefit.

Usually the concession will apply to certain days, usually matinees when there is plenty of seating available. Check at your local cinema or theatre for times when this concession is available.

SENIOR RAILCARDS

Anyone 60 years or over can save one third on Standard and First Class rail fares throughout Great Britain for twelve months, with a Senior Railcard. The card costs £24.

You can use your Railcard for both long and short trips. Better still you can use it almost anytime during the week, weekends and Public Holidays. Usually, the only restrictions are peak service times (rush hour).

Call your nearest train company telesales number. For train company telesales numbers contact National Rail Enquiries on 08457 48 49 50 (calls charged at local rate and may be recorded) or visit *www.nationalrail.co.uk*.

If you're renewing your Railcard then quote your existing Railcard number and expiry date.

Payment can be made by credit or debit card. If you purchase your Railcard from a train company telesales centre then you must allow at least 14 days for delivery.

If you're applying for the first time you'll need one of the following to prove your age:
- Birth certificate.
- Passport.
- Driving licence.
- You'll also need £24. Stations and agents accept cash, cheques, debit, credit and charge cards or postal orders.

FREE BUS PASSES

On 1st April 2008, a new National Bus Concession was introduced that allows eligible people to travel for free after 9.30am Mondays to Fridays, and anytime on Saturdays, Sundays and Public Holidays, on all the local bus services in England. To make an application, you will need to visit a Council Connect office in person. Your details will be checked and returned to you. You will receive a pass within fifteen working days but not before your sixtieth birthday.

HEATING

If you have insufficient money to cover the cost of heating within your home or other problems in this respect, it would be in your best interests to contact your local Social Services department. There are certain codes of practice in respect of electricity and gas as well as possible help from the Social Fund referred to earlier in this book.

Income Support is based on a level that is intended to cover all essential weekly expenses. Grants in respect of insulation and draught-proofing your home should help reduce fuel bills.

HOME ENERGY EFFICIENCY

See 'The Warm Front Scheme' earlier in this book.

The UK Government funds schemes providing up to £2,700 to households on certain benefits to improve their heating and energy efficiency. In England the scheme is known as Warm Front, in Northern Ireland it is Warm Homes, in Scotland it is Warm Deal and the Central Heating Programme and in Wales it is the Home Energy Efficiency Scheme.

For further information, contact Energy Action Grants Agency:
Registered Office:
EAGA plc
EAGA House, Archbold Terrace, Newcastle upon Tyne NE2 1DB

Chapter Four

Disability Benefits and Carers

DISABILITY LIVING ALLOWANCE (UNDER 65 YEARS)

This is an allowance for people who became disabled earlier than the age of sixty-five and who claimed for financial help before having reached the age of sixty-five years. It is for those who have difficulty in moving around, i.e. not able to walk or have difficulty walking, or persons who may need to be accompanied outside the home. It is for those people who may need assistance through being disabled, ill or both.

Help must have been needed for three months and still be required for a further six months. This allowance is rarely affected by savings and not influenced by NIS contributions. Certain rules apply for anyone with a terminal illness. They would receive aid promptly and the help for the three months stipulation does not apply.

Disability Living Allowance has two parts called 'components':

A **care component** – if you need help looking after yourself or supervision to keep you safe. A **mobility component** – if you can't walk or need help getting around.

Some people will be entitled to receive just one component; others may get both.

Care Component:

Weekly rate	
Highest rate	£67.00
Middle rate	£44.85
Lowest rate	£17.75

Mobility Component:

Weekly rate	
Higher rate	£46.75
Lower rate	£17.75

The Benefit Enquiry Line is open 8.30 am to 6.30 pm Monday to Friday and 9.00 am to 1.00 pm Saturday
Telephone: 0800 882 200
Textphone: 0800 243 355
You can also use the RNID Typetalk service

ATTENDANCE ALLOWANCE

The Attendance Allowance is available to persons below the age of sixty-five who are either physically disabled or disabled through mental illness. Also to people who are over sixty-five years of age and who found they were disabled or ill in some way before reaching the age of sixty-five.

Two weekly rates are available in respect of the Attendance Allowance:
Higher rate £67.00   Lower rate £44.85
The higher rate is in respect of help required during the day and at night.

Savings are not taken into consideration and neither are other remunerations. Receipt of the Attendance Allowance may entitle you to extra Income Support, Housing Benefit and Council Tax Benefit through the Severe Disability Premium.

Usually there are certain conditions to be met such as having needed help for the past six months, but with regard to being terminally ill there are special rules. Claim straight away – if you delay you may lose benefit.

You can claim online or get a claim pack by phoning the Benefit Enquiry Line. The Benefit Enquiry Line is open 8.30 am to 6.30 pm Monday to Friday and 9.00 am to 1.00 pm Saturday.

Telephone: 0800 88 22 00.: Textphone: 0800 24 33 55.

You can also use the RNID Typetalk service, or if you are on the Internet: go to: *http://www.dwp.gov.uk*.

INCAPACITY BENEFIT

The Incapacity Benefit is normally paid to women up to the age of sixty years of age and men up to the age of sixty-five, when you will start receiving Retirement Pension. Incapacity Benefit is based on NIS Contributions.

You cannot get Incapacity Benefit if you receive a state pension. However, when you reach the state pension age and are claiming Incapacity Benefit, you may choose to continue receiving Incapacity Benefit for a few further years if that is a better option. You may need to take advice on which is the best option for you. For further information:

- ☐ Go to your local Jobcentre Plus office to get a claim form.
- ☐ Claim online at *www.dwp.gov.uk/eservice/*. You can download a claim form from there.
- ☐ Or go to the local Citizens' Advice Bureau, which provides independent advice on many issues including benefits. They will be listed in the 'phone book. and also have a website: *www.citizensadvice.org.uk*.

SEVERE DISABLEMENT ALLOWANCE

You cannot make a new claim for Severe Disablement Allowance, but if you've been receiving the allowance before April 2001, you will continue to receive it.

The Severe Disablement Allowance current maximum weekly rate is £51.05 (April 2008) plus additions depending on your age. The rate usually increases each April. It is not taxable.

For further information: Benefit Enquiry Line – BEL

England, Wales and Scotland – Tel: 0800 882 200

Textphone: 0800 243 355

Northern Ireland – Tel: 0800 220 674

Textphone: 0800 243 787

THE INDEPENDENT LIVING (1993) FUND

The Independent Living (1993) Fund is a government funded trust which provides money to severely disabled people to help pay for personal care that they need. Applicants must fulfil the following criteria.

- Be aged between 16 and 65.
- Receive the highest care component of the Disability Living Allowance.
- Need to pay someone, other than a relative, to provide personal care to enable them to live at home.
- Receive Income Support or have an income, which is not enough to pay for the required care.
- Have less than £18,500 capital.
- Already receive help from Social Services, valued at £200 per week – having had regard to the client's available income.

Applications have to be made via Social Services. Forms are available from them or from the Fund.

Information leaflets are also available from the Fund.

More information can be obtained from the Customer Services Officer on the contact number below:

P O Box 7525

Nottingham NG2 4ZT

Tel: 0845 601 8815 (9.00am – 4.30pm, Monday – Wednesday; 9.00am – 2.00pm and 3.30pm – 4.30pm Thursday; 9am – 4pm Friday)

Web Site Address is: *www.ilf.org.uk*

HELP WITH NURSING HOME OR CARE HOME FEES

If this type of decision had to be made, then it would ultimately involve Social Services. It would be necessary to assess your financial situation, which would involve a means test. This test would be to ascertain if you had finances to help towards paying the fees.

If you know you want to stay in a care home, your admission can be permanent from the start. Most local authorities, however, prefer you to have a trial period to see if you like it.

The level of funding available will vary throughout the UK.

People are usually expected to pay privately for a care home if they have savings and investments of more than £22,250 in England, £21,500 in Scotland, £22,000 in Wales and £22,250 in Northern Ireland.. This includes the value of their property. There is a sliding scale of State contribution where savings are between £13,500 in England, £13,000 in Scotland, £19,000 in Wales and £13,500 in Northern Ireland. People with savings below will receive funding through Social Services.

HOW TO OBTAIN DISABILITY EQUIPMENT

This equipment is varied and includes such items as wheelchairs, bath seats, stair lifts, attached supports to help you up or down a step and also walking aids and alarm systems.

Some of the providers of this equipment are:
- your General Practitioner;
- hospitals;
- Community Care Nurses.

If in doubt, contact your local Social Services Department. There are various related benefits, including the Social Fund, charities and other sources.

Chapter Five

Retirement Pension

BASIC PENSION

At the moment, the State Pension age is 65 for men and 60 for women born on or before 5 April 1950. State Pension age for women will increase gradually from 2010, so that by 2020 it will be 65.

The increase in the State Pension age will not affect women born on or before 5 April 1950. Women born between 6 April 1950 and 5 April 1955 (inclusive) will have a State Pension age between 60 and 65. Women born on or after 6 April 1955 and before 6 April 1959 will have a State Pension age of 65.

If a married woman has not paid enough National Insurance contributions, then she can claim on her husband's contributions. However, if she has a pension based on her own contributions then she may claim on her own contributions. If a man or a woman is widowed or divorced then they may be able to get a pension or an increased pension in respect of their former partner.

Full Basic State Pension (per week from 7 April 2008):

□ Based on your own or your late husband's, wife's or civil partner's NI contributions, £90.70.

□ Full Basic State Pension for a couple is £145.05. However, your individual circumstances may affect the amount receive.

□ Based on your husband's NI contributions, £54.35.

□ Non-contributory Over 80 pension, £54.35

□ Age Addition, 25p a week paid to anyone age 80 or over in addition to their State Pension.

How much you get depends on how many qualifying years your NI contributions record contains. A qualifying year is a tax year in which you have paid sufficient contributions towards a pension. As an approximate guide, if you have 90% of your working life as qualifying years you should be eligible. If not you may be able to obtain a reduced pension and if it were possible not to draw your pension for up to five years, you would again be able to increase it.

MARRIED COUPLE'S ALLOWANCE

If you're married and you or your husband, wife or civil partner were born before 6 April 1935, you can claim Married Couple's Allowance.

You can call the Pension Service 0845 6060 265 or Textphone 0845 6060 285 , 8.00 am to 8.00 pm Monday to Friday

ADDITIONAL PENSION

Any additional pension received is based on earnings since April 1978. It is paid under the State Earnings-Related Pension Scheme – SERPS. You do not have to be receiving a basic pension to receive an additional pension. If you have taken part in a contracted-out occupational pension scheme or a personal pension scheme, your additional pension will be reduced because a contracted-out deduction will be made.

If you contributed to SERPS the maximum percentage of your SERPS pension that your widow, widower or surviving civil partner could inherit is on a sliding scale depending on when you were born and the age at which you retired.

Further information is available in The Pensions Service booklet, *Inheritance of SERPS*, which you obtain by writing to:
The Pension Service, PO Box 1005, Newcastle upon Tyne NE98 1WZ
Telephone: 0845 606 0265: Fax: 0191 218 6061
Monday to Friday, 8.00 am to 8.00 pm

GRADUATED PENSION

This is calculated by the amount of graduated NI contributions paid by you from April 1961 to April 1997. You may be able to claim a Graduated Pension even though you do not receive a Basic or Additional Pension.

PENSION CREDIT

This tops up your weekly income. Many pensioners are entitled to Pension Credit. Yet some who are eligible are not claiming it. Ensure you are not missing out. There are two parts of Pension Credit – you may be eligible to receive one or both of them:

Guarantee Credit tops up your weekly income to a guaranteed minimum level set by the Government.

Savings Credit provides up to an additional £19.71 for single people or £26.13 for couples, as a reward for having modest savings for your retirement.

You may receive a payment backdated for up to 12 months. From 6 October 2008, it is proposed to change this period from 12 months to three months. So if you want to apply for more than three months in the past, make sure you send in your application before 6 October 2008.

The term 'partner' is used to mean your husband, wife or civil partner, or the person you live with as if you are married to them or as if you are in a civil partnership with them.

To qualify

- ☐ You need to be 60 or over for Guarantee Credit; 65 or over for Savings Credit.
- ☐ Generally, you will receive Guarantee Credit if your weekly income is less than £124.05 if you are single and £189.35 if you are a couple.
- ☐ For Savings Credit, you can have a higher weekly income – normally up to around £174 if you are single or £255 if you are a couple – and still receive some benefit.
- ☐ All these amounts may be higher if you are severely disabled, a carer, or have certain housing costs.
- ☐ There is no savings limit for Pension Credit but if you have over £6,000 this will reduce the amount you get.

You can get a claim form by phoning the Pension Credit Helpline on 0800 99 1234, textphone 0800 169 0133, 8am to 8pm, Monday to Friday, or by visiting the Pension Service website.

OVER EIGHTY

Over 80 Pension is a non-contributory pension for people aged 80 or over with little or no State Pension.

You must have lived in the UK since the age of sixty. This special pension does not depend on National Insurance contributions.

You can claim the Over 80 Pension if you are:

☐ Aged 80 or over.

☐ Not getting a State Pension or you are getting less than a full State Pension because you have not paid enough National Insurance (NI) contributions.

☐ Currently living in England, Scotland or Wales.

☐ If you have lived in Great Britain for 10 years or more in any continuous period of 20 years before or after your 80th birthday.

STATE PENSION AND AGE ADDITION

If you are receiving retirement pension and have reached the age of eighty years old you will receive an extra 25p per week. Your retirement pension is automatically adjusted. If not, contact your local Social Security Office. Other benefits are varied, solely dependent upon the individual and their personal circumstances.

Further information can be obtained from your local Social Security Office, Age Concern and/or Citizens' Advice Bureau.

INVALIDITY ADDITION

If you have been receiving an age-related, long-term Incapacity Benefit before reaching pension age, you will receive extra payment on top of this amount to which you are already entitled. If receiving an additional Pension the total of Invalidity Addition will be reduced.

CARER'S ALLOWANCE

If your husband, wife or civil partner is dependent on you and you are receiving some Basic Pension, then you will be classed as a 'Carer'.

A Carer's Allowance is, at the moment of going to press, £50.55 per week, though this is affected by the other benefits you receive.

To qualify:
- You must look after someone for at least 35 hours a week;
- The person you look after must receive a qualifying disability benefit;
- If you work you must not earn more than £95;
- You must not be receiving one of a list of other benefits;
- You must be living in the UK when you claim Carer's Allowance;
- You must not be a full-time student.

You can claim Carer's Allowance if you are over 65. If your State Retirement Pension is worth more than Carer's Allowance you cannot get Carer's Allowance. However, you may still be able to get the carer addition with Pension Credit.

HOW THE RETIREMENT PENSION IS PAID

Retirement Pension is paid into your bank, post office account, or building society directly. This is the usual way State Pensions and Benefits are paid.

If you need further information about Direct Payment then contact the Pension Centre that pays your pension and/or benefits.

If you change your address, your bank details change, or any cirumstances change, then contact the Pension Centre that pays your pension and/or benefits. You will either be able to give your new details over the telephone or ask for a form to be posted to you for completion and return.

VARIATIONS IN PENSION PAYMENTS

If you are receiving Jobseeker's Allowance, Incapacity Benefit, Severe Disablement Allowance, Invalid Care Allowance or a Widow's Pension and claim State Retirement Pension, this could affect your entitlement to the other allowances. You can decide on the one that allows you to receive more money. Contact your Benefits Agency or the Citizens' Advice Bureau if you need help.

Your state pension will not change no matter how long you are in hospital but Attendance Allowance (AA) and Disability Living

Allowance (DLA) would be put on hold after 28 days. You need to let the office that pays your benefits know when you go into hospital and when you are discharged. For more information contact Age Concern, they have a leaflet titled *Going Into Hospital.*

OBTAINING INFORMATION ABOUT YOUR PENSION

It is possible to acquire a projection of what your Retirement Pension will be by contacting your local Social Security Office or Age Concern for help: 020 8765 7200.

BEREAVEMENT PAYMENTS

A Bereavement Payment is a one-off lump sum based on your late husband or wife's national insurance contributions. It used to be called Widow's Payment.

Bereavement Allowance

This a regular payment, paid for 52 weeks from the bereavement, and based on your late husband or wife's national insurance contributions. It used to be called Widow's Pension.

About The Bereavement Allowance & Bereavement Payment

This system will not affect women who were already getting benefits under the previous scheme as long as they continue to qualify under the rules.

You can claim both Bereavement Allowance and Bereavement Payment. The form comes with notes that will help you fill it in and tell you where to send the completed form.

A single tax-free lump sum of £2000 may be payable immediately to help towards costs arising from bereavement. A widow/widower may be entitled to this if his/her late spouse had paid enough National Insurance contributions and he/she was under 60 when her spouse died; or their husband/wife was not getting a Category A State Pension when he /she died.

You should claim straight away. If you delay you may lose benefit. Contact your local Social Security Office for further information or if you have access to the Internet go to: *www.dwp.gov.uk.*

Chapter Six

National Health Costs

You may be entitled to help with any of the following National Health costs, or towards part cost, if not the full cost, of travelling to hospital for National Health treatment.

- ☐ NHS prescriptions.
- ☐ NHS dental treatment.
- ☐ NHS Sight tests.
- ☐ Glasses and contact lenses.
- ☐ Necessary costs of travel to receive NHS treatment under the care of a consultant, or through a referral by a doctor or dentist.
- ☐ NHS wigs and fabric supports.

Note: 'fabric supports' means spinal or abdominal supports or surgical brassieres supplied through a hospital.

It is possible to obtain information through your local Social Security Office, hospital, dental surgery, doctor's surgery or from an optician.

NHS TRAVEL COSTS

You can get help with necessary travel costs to receive NHS treatment under the care of a consultant, or through a referral by a doctor or dentist if you or your partner receives any of the following:

- ☐ Income Support.
- ☐ Income-based Jobseeker's Allowance. *Incapacity Benefit or Disability Living Allowance do not count as they are not income related.*
- ☐ Pension Credit Guarantee Credit.
- ☐ If you are entitled to, or named on, a valid NHS tax credit exemption certificate.
- ☐ If you are a war pensioner and the treatment is for your accepted disability.
- ☐ Partial help: if you are named on a valid HC3 certificate.

Note: If you would like to find out if the NHS Low Income scheme can help you, collect a HC1 form (claim for help with health costs) from a Jobcentre Plus office or NHS hospital. Your dentist or optician may have copies too, or telephone: 0845 610 1112.

EYE SIGHT TESTS

☐ You will receive help with costs, if you are over forty and the brother, sister, parent or child of a glaucoma patient

☐ If you have diabetes.

If you are registered as partially sighted or a blind person.

Hospital Eye Service patients requiring intricate lenses.

If you are a recipient of Income Support, Family Credit or in a low income group

To receive help, complete a form at the Opticians. Your optician, doctor or Social Services will be able to advise you.

Recipients of War/MOD Disablement Pension, who need treatment because of injury for which Disablement Pension is received, should contact the War Pensions Agency, DSS, Norcross, Blackpool, FY5 3WP. See Department of Health Leaflet HC11 *Help with health costs*.

GLASSES AND CONTACT LENSES

Help will be available towards the cost of glasses and contact lenses if you come under any of the following categories:

☐ If you receive Income Support or Family Credit.

☐ If you have a certificate supplied by the Health Benefits Division.

☐ If you are a Hospital Eye Service patient, having paid for the initial pair and needing a continual change of spectacles.

☐ If you are in receipt of a War/MOD Disablement Pension, needing spectacles due to an injury for which Disablement Pension is received.

☐ If an intricate lense or lenses are required.

Ask your Optician for information or get in touch with your local Social Security Office.

Persons claiming a War Pension should contact the War Pensions Agency, DSS, Norcross, Blackpool, FY5 3WP.

FREE HEARING AIDS

This facility encompasses both senior citizens and all other age groups with a hearing problem. The batteries for the hearing aids are also supplied free of charge. Replacement batteries are available either from the hospital (a mailing service) or from your doctor's surgery.

If you feel you need this type of hearing aid help, consult your doctor's surgery and a hospital appointment will be arranged.

WIGS AND FABRIC SUPPORTS

You can obtain help in respect of cost, if you are supplied with a wig or fabric support as a patient within a hospital or if you are receiving Income Support, Family Credit or are within a low income group. This also applies if you receive War/MOD Disablement Pension and need Wigs and/or Fabric Supports due to an injury for which you receive the Disability Pension.

You will receive free wigs and fabric supports or help with costs. A list of some of the National Health Scheme Wigs and Fabric Supports is as below:

- Stock modacrylic wig
- Partial wig – human hair
- Full bespoke wig – human hair
- Abdominal support
- Spinal support
- Surgical brassiere

To obtain further information, either contact your doctor's surgery or your local Social Security Office.

PRESCRIPTIONS

If you are sixty years of age or over then you are eligible for free prescriptions. Other eligible groups are people with certain stipulated medical conditions and those who receive a War/MOD Disablement Pension who need prescriptions for treatment because of the injury for which a Disablement Pension is received. Those who receive Income support, Family Credit or are in a low income group are also eligible.

Those from lower income groups under sixty years of age must obtain a claim form from their doctor or from a local Social Security Office.

If you are pregnant or have had a child in the past year you are entitled to free prescriptions. Get form FW8 from your doctor, midwife or health visitor to apply for a Maternity Exemption Certificate. The form is sent off to the Prescription Pricing Authority who will issue the certificate.

For further information get in touch with your local Citizens' Advice Bureau.

PRESCRIPTION SEASON TICKETS

If you do not qualify for free prescriptions you may be able to reduce the cost by buying a Prescription Prepayment Certificate ('season ticket') from the Prescription Pricing Authority. This certificate will cover the cost of all your prescriptions during a particular period.

For instance, if you have to pay for more than 14 items in 12 months, you could save money by buying a Prescription Prepayment Certificate. As from April 2008, the charge for a single prescription item (at the time of going to press) is £7.10.

☐ A 3-month Prescription Prepayment Certificate will cost £27.85.

☐ A 12-month Prescription Prepayment Certificate will cost £102.50

You can apply for a Prescription Prepayment Certificate by completing form FP95, which you obtain from pharmacies or your doctor's surgery.

If you have Internet access go to *www.ppa.org.uk*.

Telephone – 0845 850 0030 – have a credit or debit card to hand.

If you had to pay for your prescription whilst waiting for your Prescription Prepayment Certificate, as long as you have a receipt, you can get a refund. The receipt is form FP57. You obtain this from the pharmacist where your prescription was dispensed. This has to be sorted out at the time, as you will not be able to obtain it later. Fill the receipt form in and send it off to claim the refund.

FREE HOSPITAL MEDICINES

If you are in hospital as a National Health Scheme patient or are a National Health Scheme patient leaving the hospital you are able to obtain free medicines.

SERVICE TO HELP WITH INCONTINENCE

Many disabled people have trouble with either occasional or regular incontinence, which can be costly. The help available and how it is administered will vary from one area to another. It is important that you seek advice from an NHS continence adviser as to what help is available with laundry services and disposal of waste.

FREE HOSPITAL APPLIANCES

You can probably obtain free hospital appliances if you are a patient in a National Health Hospital. Day or out patients within a low income bracket or who are receiving Income Support or Family Credit may either get free appliances or help towards their cost. Those who receive a War Disablement Pension needing appliances because of their disability may also receive help.

DENTAL TREATMENT

You are entitled to help or free dental treatment if you are receiving Income Support, Family Credit or are within a low-income group. In addition, there may also be help for those who receive a War/MOD Disablement Pension, who need dental treatment because of the injury for which their Disablement Pension is received.

You receive this entitlement by informing your dentist that you require free treatment. If you are registered for Continuing Care with your dentist, you can ask for a treatment plan. This plan would be provided free of charge and explain the treatment recommended.

If you are on a low income, obtain the entitlement by filling in a claim form, which is available either through the dentist or your Social Security Office. War Pensioners claim by settling the dentist account and sending the receipt to: Treatment Group, War Pensions Agency, DSS, Norcross, Blackpool GY5 3WP. For further information contact your local Social Security Office or dentist.

CONTINUING HEALTH CARE

There are those who may need continuing care before or following a stay in hospital and it may be possible to receive this if you live in your own home, a residential home, nursing home or sheltered housing.

Further information under such circumstances can be obtained through Social Services or if necessary Age Concern.

FOOT CARE

If you apply through your General Practitioner, you should receive treatment from a chiropodist free of charge. Chiropodists usually hold clinics in surgeries, hospitals or health centres. Sometimes chiropodists visit your home. If you need transport or cannot find the information you require in this respect, get in touch with your local Social Services Department or contact:

The Society of Chiropodists & Podiatrists
Registered Office
1 Fellmonger's Path, Tower Bridge Road , London SE1 3LY
Tel: 020 7234 8620: Fax: 0845 450 3721

DEAF AND DEAFENED PERSONS

There are services that give a wide variety of help for those who have a hearing impairment. Specialist workers, skilled in sign language, help the deaf and deafened as well as their families and carers. They provide advice on welfare rights, counselling, assessment for hearing aids and adaptations as well as other support services.

There is an organisation called the BDA (British Deaf Association). They use the British Sign Language (BSL) and it is Britain's most widely used language after English, Gaelic and Welsh.

The BDA's prime objective is to progress and to protect the interests of the deaf community and to ensure a greater enlightenment of your rights and responsibilities in society.

It promotes the idea that deaf people are looked upon as first class citizens and equal partners in society at all times and that they are an integral part of British life with equal access and opportunity.

If you have a computer with Internet access, SEARCH and find British Deaf Association (type this in full) and you will find lots of helpful information on the site.

If you need computer lessons and are on Income Support, you should be able to obtain FREE tuition at your local Community Education Centre.

Library Services often supply sub-titled (and/or signing) videos for people with hearing difficulties.

VISUALLY IMPAIRED PERSONS

There are benefits and concessions for those who are registered as partially sighted as well as for those who are registered as blind. There are local contacts, national contacts and taped literature services.

Some of the benefits and concessions for people registered as partially sighted are a free National Health Scheme sight test, a Rail Card through your local railway operator and exemption from Directory Enquiry charges on the telephone.

Magnifiers can be provided. Also available is an additional housing benefit or a reduction in Council Tax, special aids and equipment for work and free postage under 'Articles for the Blind' labels. Additionally, special arrangements can be made for voting through the local council.

It is possible to use a computer and training is available.

The best people to contact are at the Royal National Institute of Blind People, who will help even if you only have a slight problem of impaired eyesight.

Their Helpline (telephone 0845 766 9999 / 020 7388 2525) offers an immediate, expert and confidential service. Many of their Helpline staff have sight problems themselves. They are trained to listen and to give reassurance and advice.

The staff can:
- put you in touch with specialist advice services
- give you details of support groups and services in your area

They will provide you with free information on:
- eye conditions
- making the most of your remaining vision – magnifiers, lighting
- registering as blind or partially sighted
- benefits and your rights
- living with sight loss

The Help line is open Monday to Friday 9.00am – 5.00pm., except Wednesdays when it is open from 9.00am – 4.00pm. Messages can be left on their answer phone outside these hours.

Interpreters can be arranged for most languages.

All calls are treated in confidence even though they may be recorded, or listened-in to for quality and training purposes.

Their main address is:

Royal National Institute of Blind People
105 Judd Street, London WC1H 9NE
Tel: 020 7388 1266: Fax: 020 7388 2034

Chapter Seven

Injury Compensation

This applies to any person, no matter what their age. If an injury was sustained when you were carrying out your work and the accident was caused through negligence, your employer should pay the compensation. Obviously, the Health and Safety officials would be involved in assessing the accident

Any compensation would be dependent upon the extent of your injuries and the magnitude of negligence. For further information, ask at your local Citizens' Advice Bureau, a solicitor or your Trade Union.

The Social Services would also be able to advise you of related benefits. These would depend upon your financial circumstances and on the extent of your injury or injuries.

INDUSTRIAL INJURIES DISABLEMENT BENEFIT

The amount of benefit you get depends on:
- your age
- the seriousness of your disability – assessed by a doctor on a scale of one to 100 per cent

INDUSTRIAL INJURIES DISABLEMENT BENEFIT (ACCIDENTS)

The table below is a guide only:

Assessed level of disablement	Weekly Over 18	Weekly Under 18
100%	£136.80	£83.85
90%	£123.12	£75.47
80%	£109.44	£67.08

Assessed level of disablement	Weekly Over 18	Weekly Under 18
70%	£95.76	£58.70
60%	£82.08	£50.31
50%	£68.40	£41.93
40%	£54.72	£33.54
30%	£41.04	£25.16
20%	£27.36	£16.77

Industrial Injuries Disablement Benefit and related benefits are paid into your bank, building society, Post Office or a National Savings account that accepts Direct Payment.

If you are disabled by disease or deafness caused by your work, you may be able to claim other benefits. Some may be taken into account as income for means-tested benefits.

OTHER INDUSTRIAL INJURIES BENEFITS

Pneumoconiosis and Byssinosis Assessment

You are able to claim if you are unable to return to your usual work or work with similar pay because of an accident or disease caused by employment that happened before 1 October 1990.

Assessed level of disablement	Weekly
11% to 19%	£27.36
1% to 10%	£13.68

Mesothelioma Assessment

Mesothelioma Assessment is paid at 100 per cent (£136.80) from the outset of the claim, without the need for the 90-day waiting period

EXCEPTIONALLY SEVERE DISABLEMENT ALLOWANCE

You can claim £54.80 paid in addition to the Constant Attendance

Allowance rates, if you're assessed at Constant Attendance Allowance intermediate or exceptional rate and need permanent, constant care and attention.

REDUCED EARNINGS ALLOWANCE

You may be able to get Reduced Earnings Allowance if your current earnings, or earnings in a job which it is considered you could do, are less than the current earnings in your previous regular occupation. You can only get this if your accident occurred before 1 October 1990. The maximum weekly rate is £54.72.

RETIREMENT ALLOWANCE

Retirement Allowance replaces Reduced Earnings Allowance when you reach State Pension age. The maximum weekly rate is £13.68.

You can claim Industrial Injuries Disablement Benefit straight away by completing a form at your Jobcentre Plus office, or by downloading the claim form from the link below.

http://www.direct.gov.uk/en/Diol1/DoItOnline/DG_4017784

WAR DISABLEMENT PENSION

If you are no longer serving in HM Armed Forces and your claimed disablement arose before 6 April 2005 it is possible that you may be able to claim War Disablement Pension under the War Pensions Scheme. That is if you've been injured or disabled during a time of war or as a result of service in Her Majesty's Armed Forces.

You can claim if you were injured or disabled through serving in HM Armed Forces, including the:

- Ulster Defence Regiment (now known as the Royal Irish Regiment)
- Home Guard
- Nursing and auxiliary services
- Civil defence volunteer (CDV)
- Merchant navy
- Naval auxiliary

- ☐ Coastguard

If you were disabled because of an injury you received or a disease you suffered because:

- ☐ of conditions during a war
- ☐ you were a prisoner-of-war

If, during the Second World War

- ☐ you were a civilian injured or disabled as a result of enemy action
- ☐ you were a member of the Polish Forces under British Command (or you were in the Polish Resettlement Forces) and were injured or disabled in service

If disablement was caused by Service in HM Armed Forces on or after 6 April 2005, claims should be made under the Armed Forces Compensation Scheme. To obtain the War Disablement Pension contact: War Pensions Agency, DSS, Norcross, Blackpool FY5 3WP.

Free Veterans Helpline: 0800 169 22 77.

WAR PENSIONS SCHEME

The War Pensions Scheme is for ex-Service personnel whose injuries, wounds and illnesses arose prior to 6 April 2005.

This scheme also covers War Widows and Widowers Pensions.

CONSTANT ATTENDANCE ALLOWANCE

If you need daily care and attention because of a disability and you claim Industrial Injuries Disablement Benefit or a War Disablement Pension, you can claim Constant Attendance Allowance.

If you're claiming Industrial Injuries Disablement Benefit, to claim Constant Attendance Allowance, you must need daily care and attention (for example, home nursing or home meals) and your disability must have been assessed at 100 per cent. You can contact your local Jobcentre Plus office to find out if you're eligible to claim Constant Attendance Allowance.

The Constant Attendance Allowance rate you're paid is based on a doctor's assessment of your needs.

Constant Attendance	Weekly
Exceptional rate	£109.60
Intermediate rate	£82.20
Normal maximum rate	£54.80
Part-time rate	£27.40

To claim Constant Attendance Allowance if you are claiming War Disablement Pension you must need personal help for the same reasons that you get a war pension and be getting a war pension of 80 per cent or more. To find out if you're eligible to claim Constant Attendance Allowance, you can contact the Service Personnel and Veterans Agency helpline on:

Telephone: 0800 169 2277 or Textphone: 0800 169 3458

The helpline is open from 8.15 am to 5.15 pm Monday to Thursday, and 8.15 am to 4.30 pm on Fridays.

FOR SPECIFIED MINOR INJURIES

There is a varying scale in respect of the Specified Minor Injuries Allowance. It is assessed by taking into consideration just how important the injury is in relation to the rest of that part of the body. If, for example, you injured your little finger, this may not be considered as important as that of your index finger. In addition, if you injured a finger and a toe, which injury would be considered the most important? Although the scale differs in respect of multiple losses, there is no difference in the gratuity received regardless of whether or not you were a private or officer in the armed forces. Therefore, the gratuity depends on the extent of the injury or injuries.

Related benefits would depend solely on the extent of the disability or disabilities.

All War Pensions should be claimed by getting in touch with the War Pensions Agency, DSS Norcross, Blackpool FY5 3WP.

Chapter Eight

Holidays and Insurance

Certain welfare groups, which are run for senior citizens, arrange holidays at a very low cost, although not all are suitable for those with a disability. The types of holiday vary quite widely.

Some, though not all, local social service departments also have holiday accommodation facilities set up for the elderly and disabled and may provide finance for holidays.

Age Concern will have information on free or very low cost holidays 0808 800 6565 (Textphone-Minicom 0800 26 96 26) 0808 808 7575

A lot of older people live alone and often isolation can be a real problem – especially for those who live on a low income. For people who have not had a holiday for many years and have no possibility of arranging or paying for one the benefits of a National Benevolent Fund for the Aged (NBFA) holiday are invaluable. Contact: NBFA on info@nbfa.org.uk or phone 020 7828 0200 if you would like any further information.

HOLIDAY CARE SERVICE

This is a registered charity that provides information on holidays and travel for Senior Citizens and those who are disabled.

Below is a list of other charities which can help with holidays:

3H FUND

3H Fund organises subsidised group holidays for physically disabled people accompanied by volunteer carers, providing a break from the routine of caring for the carer or family of that person.

147A Camden Road, Tunbridge Wells, Kent TN1 2RA
Telephone: 01892 547 474: Fax 01892 524 703

accessatlast

Accesstalast provides a booking service for accessible holiday accommodation and services in Britain and abroad.

18 Hazel Grove, Tarleton, Preston, Lancashire PR4 6DQ
Telephone: 01772 814 555 : Fax 0845 890 2119

BREAK

BREAK supports children, adults and families with special care needs - including supported holidays, short breaks, respite care and day care support.

Davison House,
1 Montague Road, Sheringham, Norfolk NR26 8WN
Telephone: 01263 822 161 : Fax: 01263 822 181

ENABLE HOLIDAYS

Enable Holidays is a travel agency offering a range of accessible overseas holidays for wheelchair users and people with limited mobility, their families and friends.

26 The Green, Kings Norton, Birmingham B38 8SD
Telephone: 08712 224 939 : Fax: 08712 225 753

GROOMS HOLIDAYS

Grooms Holidays is the part of the Grooms-Shaftesbury charity that provides accessible holiday locations in England at affordable rates. Accommodation includes both serviced and self-catering.

50 Scrutton St, London EC2A 4XQ
Telephone: 020 7452 2000: Fax: 020 7452 2001

HANDICAPPED AID TRUST

The Handicapped Aid Trust gives grants towards the cost of helpers to assist disabled people on holiday, and towards the cost of holidays and helpers to give carers a break.

Windmill House, Church Road, Lytham, Lancashire
Telephone: 01253 796 441

NATIONAL RAIL

National Rail – provides information on services for disabled or mobility-impaired passengers on the national rail network.
Enquiries: 08457 484 950: Text telephone: 08456 050 600

PHAB ENGLAND

Phab England is a charity promoting the coming together of people with and without physical disabilities. This includes organising residential weeks and short stays for disabled and non-disabled young people at fully accessible activity centres.
Summit House, 50 Wandle Road, Croydon, Surrey CR0 1DF
Telephone: 020 8667 9443 : Fax: 020 8681 1399

PETS AND INSURANCE

Pets can be our best friends, yet it may be that when it comes to paying a vet's bill, money is scarce.

Help The Aged, on their Internet web site, send people to a company named the **Intune Group Limited**, in respect of Insuring Pets. Their telephone number is: 0800 022 3193, a freephone number. An adviser at Intune will, after a recorded message, answer your call.

Among many other things, the Intune Group tell you that their Pet Insurance is provided by the **Liverpool Victoria Insurance Company Limited**. With regard to the Liverpool Victoria Insurance Company Limited web site, you will only obtain a 10% discount IF you obtain a quote on line. Their web site address is: *https://www.lvpet.co.uk/pet/schemes*. To obtain a quote, from Liverpool Victoria Insurance, other than via the Internet, telephone: 0800 022 3906 and quote offer code **IELO**. This is what you will receive if you take a pet Insurance out with Liverpool Victoria Insurance Company Limited:

☐ Up to £5,000 cover per condition for vets' fees.
  • Essential pet insurance – for a maximum of 12 months treatment for each condition.
  • Premier pet insurance – no time limit for treatment for each condition.

- No upper age limit for your pet.
- No instalment charge if you wish to pay monthly.
- UK based call centres and access to 4 helplines.
- Automatic cover for a range of benefits including advertising costs if your pet gets lost or stolen and holiday cancellation costs if your pet needs emergency treatment.
- You must own the pet, be 18 years or older and a UK resident.
- Your pet must not be less than eight weeks old.
- Your pet must not fall under the restrictions of the Dangerous Dogs Act 1991, the Dogs (Northern Ireland) Order 1983, Dogs (Northern Ireland) Act 1991 or any changes to those laws.
- You need to have all your pet's details to hand, including their medical history. Note: If your dog is rescued or for some unknown reason you haven't this information, you will find them very helpful.

The People's Dispensary for Sick Animals (PDSA), is a charity run on voluntary contributions. You can get help, free of charge, for your animals at the PDSA branch in your area. If you can, though, make a small contribution, as it will be gratefully received.

Contact details are listed at the end of this book.

Sometimes it becomes difficult to walk a dog and I have heard of people finding their much-loved pet a new home because of this. Pets are very special to us and I suggest that if you do find it difficult to walk your dog, you give your local schools a call to see if there might be a volunteer or get hold of one of your local charitable organisations, for example, The Round Table, Ladies Circle, Rotary or Inner Wheel and ask them for help in this respect.

CAR INSURANCE

The majority of car insurances have to be paid for by the car only and once you reach sixty-five or sixty-six years of age, it can go up. Premium Rates may become higher due to your age. Age Concern offers Motor Insurance, and they believe the older you become the more careful you are with your possessions. So, they are worth telephoning to obtain an estimate: Freephone Information Line 0800 00 99 66.

Chapter Nine

Further Information on Community Care

The aim of Community Care is to ensure that the services given by the local authorities and health authorities sustain the people within the community; that they are provided to those people who require them most of all and that the actual services meet the individual person's actual needs.

The quality of care is important and this has to be checked and is checked by the use of inspection units, which set specifications for the services provided. Contracts for care are monitored. Complaints procedures have been introduced and the local authorities utilise other organisations to provide assistance, so that it is not totally provided by them.

There are Assessment and Care Management Teams within Social Services. If you have a problem, please do not feel that there is no one out there to help you. Make a telephone call, either to the Social Services or Citizens' Advice Bureau. Local telephone numbers are in your telephone directory or telephone Directory Enquiries.

Here is a list of some of the services within your Community:

- ☐ Community Mental Health for Older People
- ☐ Sensory Impairment
- ☐ Drug Users
- ☐ HIV Injection, AIDS and families
- ☐ Council Environmental Services
- ☐ Women and Children subjected to Domestic Violence

There are many other services – always ask your GP, your community nurse or Social Services.

LEGAL AID

Plans for six new Community Legal Advice services were announced on the 29 May 2008. Six new areas in England and Wales have been identified to gain improved civil legal aid and advice services in plans unveiled by the Legal Services Commission (LSC). So please, if you have legal problems, which may be through no fault of your own, get in touch with your local Citizens' Advice Bureau to find out the details.

These are some of the problems for which you may need Legal Aid:

- ☐ Accidents
- ☐ Buying goods
- ☐ Claims
- ☐ Criminal cases
- ☐ Debt
- ☐ Divorce
- ☐ Eviction
- ☐ Family and children

If you live or work in the catchment area of a law centre, contact the law centre to see if they can help. Law centres can give benefits advice as well as help in other areas of the law.

Under the Community Legal Service Help scheme anyone who receives Income Support or Income-based Jobseeker's Allowance automatically qualifies for free legal advice, if his or her capital is below the set limit. Other people, in or out of work may qualify if their savings and income are low enough.

Not all solicitors are a part of this scheme, only those who are contracted with the Legal Services Commission (they will probably have a CLS logo in their window). Look in the CLS directory in a local library or ask your local Citizens' Advice Bureau.

COMPLAINTS PROCEDURE

If you feel that you have been assessed unfairly by the Local Authority Social Services under the National Health Service and Community Care Act 1990 and you are quite sure that you do need help, then you have the right to complain.

There is a complaints procedure. If this seems unsatisfactory, then you can go to The Ombudsman. You can make this complaint directly to The Ombudsman or through a councillor, but you must make your complaint within twelve months of the date you realised you had a complaint to make. You obtain The Ombudsman's address through your local council, library, or your Citizens' Advice Bureau.

You may feel the council had a duty to provide you with a service that it did not provide you with, or that it withdrew it unfairly. Either you or someone on your behalf can report this to the Secretary of State for Health (Local Authority Social Services Act 1970 as amended by section 50 of the National Health Service and Community Care Act 1990). Consulting a solicitor before doing this would be wise.

There is also an Appeal through the courts. Again, you would need to consult a solicitor. Depending on your income, you may be entitled to legal aid. You would have to prove that the council has breached its statutory duty and this may be difficult to do. For further advice and/or an explanation with regard to complaints, contact:

RADAR (Royal Association for Disability and Rehabilitation)
12 City Forum, 250 City Road, London EC1V 8AF
Telephone: 020 7250 3222 : Textphone Minicom 020 7250 4119
Fax: 020 7250 0212
Email address : radar@radar.org.uk
or ask for advice at your Citizens' Advice Bureau.

DEPRESSION

Depression is something which can happen at anytime during one's life and getting older does not, unfortunately, take it away, but it is not a part of growing older.

Everyone gets depressed at some time or another. Naturally, there are many reasons for feeling depressed: physical illness, or perhaps the death of someone close to you – your spouse, partner, a relative, perhaps a friend. Severe depression can interfere with sleep patterns, which in turn makes us feel truly miserable and in extreme circumstances this may lead to thoughts of suicide. Very often detecting a single cause is difficult, but it needs dealing with and help must be found.

The disheartened often find it impossible to hold a conversation with a member of the family, or a friend and are unable to discuss the cause and effect of depression, so outside help can be better.

Similarly, sufferers of anxiety and anxiety attacks, find identifying the cause and taking steps to deal with the problem, is not easy. Nevertheless, sharing the problem with a close friend or relative is very important. Do not try to cope alone.

It would be advisable for someone suddenly experiencing severe depression to seek medical help. Why allow the ability to enjoy life, enjoy doing things and enjoy the company of others to be spoilt by sadness and depression? Medical advice and help may encompass advice on conquering these feelings, perhaps with the assistance of antidepressants.

If you have a friend or relative who seems exceptionally depressed and may have mentioned suicide, yet they will not consult a doctor or any other professional, it may be worth having a word with this person's doctor or health visitor. Never shrug off the seriousness of depression – someone suffering in this way would be unable to climb out of it alone, in the same way that someone having had a severe heart attack could not recover unaided.

For those who are hesitant about taking antidepressants, it would be a good idea to get in touch with a General Practitioner who specialises in homoeopathy. Names, addresses and telephone numbers can be found in Yellow Pages. There are also a few homoeopathic hospitals that would be only too pleased to put you in touch with the right General Practitioner.

MIND (National Association For Mental Health) have lots of information:

Fact sheets and booklets by subject

Booklets by series

Booklet translations

List of fact sheets

These are available by going on to their web site:

http://www.mind.org.uk/Information/
or by telephoning the Mind information line, Monday to Friday, 9.15am
to 5.15pm: 0845 766 0163

The telephone number and address of the local branch of the
Samaritan organisation can be found in the telephone directory.

To help combat MINOR depression and get a more positive
outlook:

- ☐ Be aware of why you are feeling depressed and try to be more
   optimistic about the future.
- ☐ Be positive and focus on the positive experiences within your life.
- ☐ Each day make a list of your positive achievements.
- ☐ Mix with people and socialise by joining a club or an evening class;
   learn something new.
- ☐ Each week draw up a list of all your daily activities.
- ☐ Begin that hobby. Learn that new language.
- ☐ Exercise daily.
- ☐ Learn a relaxation technique. Relax when you feel tense.
- ☐ Volunteering to help others will keep you active.
- ☐ Set a few sensible goals.
- ☐ Focus on your own uniqueness. You have skills to share with
   others.
- ☐ Focus on your past positive accomplishments.
- ☐ Focus on your future positive accomplishments.

Appendix I

Useful Information About Charities

Help The Aged
Website: *http://www.helptheaged.org.uk/en-gb/WhatWeDo/*
England: 207-221 Pentonville Road, London N1 9UZ
Tel: 020 7278 1114: Fax: 020 7278 1116
Scotland: 11 Granton Square, Edinburgh EH5 1HX
Tel: 0131 551 6331: Fax: 0131 551 5415
Wales: 12 Cathedral Rd, Cardiff CF11 9LJ
Tel: 02920 346 550: Fax: 02920 390 898
N Ireland: Ascot House, Shaftesbury Square, Belfast BT2 7DB
Tel: 02890 230 666: Fax: 02890 248 183
Email: infoni@helptheaged.org.uk

Friends Of The Elderly & Gentlefolks Help
The aim of this charity is to aid in the relief of poverty and help provide accommodation for the elderly:
40-42 Ebury Street, Westminster, London SW1W 0LZ
Telephone: 020 77308263: Fax: 020 72590154
Web Site: *www.fote.org.uk*

RETHINK
This is a charity which is concerned with supporting people with mental health problems:
Milward House, 1 Bristol Road, Keynsham, Somerset
Tel/Fax: 0117 986 4706
Email: carerbanes@rethink.org
Web site: *www.rethink.org*

PDSA
Head Office,
Whitechapel Way, Priorslee, Telford, Shropshire TF2 9PQ
Enquiries: 0800 731 2502

CHARITIES WHICH CAN ADVISE YOU ON HOLIDAYS

Arthritis Care
Arthritis Care, 18 Stephenson Way, London NW1 2HD
Email: Info@arthritiscare.org.uk: Telephone: 020 7380 6500
If you would like an information pack about Arthritis Care and the
services they offer, ring the 24-hour information line: 0845 600 6868.

British Deaf Association Offices
British Deaf Association North
13 Wilson Patten Street, Warrington, Cheshire, WA1 1PG
Email: north@bda.org.uk: Videophone IP: 81.6.233.219
Telephone: 01925 414649: Textphone: 01925 642659
Fax: 01925 652526
Deaf Association of Northern Ireland
Suite 3, Cranmore House , 611b Lisburn Road, Belfast BT9 7GT
Email: northernireland@bda.org.uk: Videophone IP: 217.41.30.182
Telephone: 02890 387700: Textphone: 02890 387706
Fax: 02890 387707
British Deaf Association Midlands
10th Floor, Coventry Point, Market Way, Coventry CV1 1EA
Email: midlands@bda.org.uk: Videophone IP: 84.12.97.143
Telephone: 02476 550936: Textphone: 02476 550393
Fax: 02476 221541
Deaf Association Wales
British Sign Language Cultural Centre,
47 Newport Road, Cardiff CF24 0AD
Email: wales@bda.org.uk
Telephone: 0845 1302851: Textphone: 0845 1302853
Fax: 0845 1302852

Scottish Deaf Association
Central Chambers, Suite 58, 93 Hope Street, Glasgow G2 6LD
Email: scotland@bda.org.uk
Telephone/Textphone: 0141 248 5554

Diabetes UK
Central Office
Macleod House, 10 Parkway, London NW1 7AA
Tel 020 7424 1000: Fax 020 7424 1001
Email info@diabetes.org.uk

British Red Cross
UK Office, 44 Moorfields, London EC2Y 9AL
Tel: 0844 871 11 11 : Fax: 020 7562 2000

The Disabled Driver's Association
Ashwellthorpe, Norwich NR16 1EX
Telephone: 0870 770 3333
Website: *http://www.dda.org.uk*

RADAR National Key Scheme (NKS)
RADAR's National Key Scheme (NKS) offers independent access
to disabled people to around 7,000 locked public toilets around the
country. Keys can be bought from RADAR at a small non-profit
charge.

RADAR National Key Scheme (NKS)
12 City Forum, 250 City Road, London EC1V 8AF
Telephone: 020 7250 3222 : Textphone Minicom 020 7250 4119
Fax: 020 7250 0212
Email address: radar@radar.org.uk

Multiple Sclerosis Society
MS National Centre
372 Edgware Road, London NW2 6ND
Tel: 020 8438 0700: Fax: 020 8438 0701

Parkinson's Disease Society
215 Vauxhall Bridge Road, London SW1V 1EJ
Helpline 0808 800 0303

Royal National Institute for the Blind
Helpline on 0845 766 9999 / 020 7388 2525

Vitalize
Short Break Bookings Team
Shap Road Industrial Estate, Shap Road
Kendal , Cumbria LA9 6NZ
Tel: 0845 345 1970 : Fax: 01539 735 567

Appendix II

National Contacts for the Blind and Partially Sighted

Royal National Institute for the Blind
Telephone No: Helpline 0845 766 9999 / 020 7388 2525

Partially Sighted Society
Queen's Road, Doncaster, South Yorkshire DN1 2NX
Tel: 01302 323132 / 01302 368998

Action for Blind People
Freephone Helpline: 0800 915 4666

LOOK
LOOK National Office,
c/o Queen Alexandra College,
49 Court Oak Road, Harborne, Birmingham B17 9TG
Telephone: 0121 428 5038
Email: admin@look-uk.org

British Association for Sporting and Creational Activity for the Blind
www.britishblindsport.org.uk

Guide Dogs for the Blind Association
The Guide Dogs for the Blind Association
Burghfield Common, Reading RG7 3YG
Tel: 0118 983 5555 : Fax: 0118 983 5433
Email: guidedogs@guidedogs.org.uk

Association of Blind African Caribbean
1st Floor, Gloucester House
8 Camberwell New Road, London SE5 0TA
Tel: 020 7735 3400: Fax: 020 7582 8334
Web: *www.obac.org.uk*
Telephone: 9.30am – 5.30pm, Monday – Friday

RNIB Talking Book Service
RNIB National Library Service (or RNIB Talking Book Service)
PO Box 173, Peterborough PE2 6WS
Telephone: 0845 762 6843 or 01733 37 53 50
Email: cservices@rnib.org.uk

The Talking Newspaper Association
T.N.A.U.K
National Recording Centre, Heathfield, East Sussex TN21 8DB .
Telephone: 01435 866102: Fax: 01435 865422
Email: info@tnauk.org.uk

Weekend Listener
National Library for the Blind
Far Cromwell Road, Bredbury, Stockport SK6 2SG
Tel: 0161 355 2000
Email: visugate.enquiries@nlbuk.org

The International Glaucoma Association
Woodcote House,
15 Highpoint Business Village
Henwood, Ashford, Kent TN24 8DH
Telephone: +44 (0)1233 64 81 70
Administration: +44 (0)1233 64 81 64
Fax: +44 (0)1233 64 81 79
Email: info@iga.org.uk

Appendix III

Useful Names & Addresses Concerning Holidays

Cosmos
> Sales & administration: National Call Centre
> Dale House, Tiviot Dale, Stockport, Cheshire SK1 1TB

> Head office:
> Wren Court, 17 London Road, Bromley, Kent BR1 1DE

Saga Holidays Ltd,
> The Saga Building, Enbrook Park, Folkestone, Kent CT20 3SE

Travel Companions
> Battlefield Tours
> Telephone: 0845 408 57 87

Appendix IV

Contacts Concerning Rented Accommodation

The National Federation of Housing Associations
Lion Court , 25 Procter Street , London WC1V 6NY
Telephone: 020 7067 1010: Fax: 020 7067 1011

The National Association of Almshouses
The Almshouse Association
Billingbear Lodge
Maidenhead Road, Wokingham, Berkshire RG40 5RU
Tel: 01344 452922: Fax: 01344 862062
E-mail: naa@almshouses.org: Website: www.almshouses.org

The Housing Corporation
Maple House, 149 Tottenham Court Road, London W1T 7BN
National telephone number : 0845 230 7000: Fax: 020 7393 2111

Royal British Legion Housing Association
http://www.britishlegion.org.uk/
Anchor Housing Association
Anchor Trust, 2nd Floor, 25 Bedford Street, London, WC2E 9ES
Tel: 020 7759 9100 : Fax: 020 7759 9101

The Abbeyfield Society
Abbeyfield House, 53 Victoria Street, St Albans, Herts AL1 3UW
Tel: 01727 857536: Fax: 01727 846168

Servite Houses Limited
2 Bridge Avenue, Hammersmith , London W6 9JP
Tel: 020 8307 3300: Fax: 020 8563 7099

Appendix V

Education and Employment

RETIREMENT

Certain employers provide talks and discussions on retirement. In addition, there are groups and organisations which hold courses. Names and addresses of three groups follow:

Retirement Education Services Limited
16 St Mary's Street, Wallingford, OXON OX10 0EW
Telephone: 01491 833696 : Fax: 01491 839913

Six Steps
Aviva plc
PO Box 48, King's House, 15 Surrey Street, Norwich NR1 3TA
Telephone 01603 687202

Laterlife Learning
Open and In-House Retirement Courses
www.retirement-courses.co.uk
Phone: 0118 983 6198: Fax: 0118 983 1425
email: learn@laterlife.com

ADULT EDUCATION

The University of the Third Age
Old Municipal Buildings
19 East Street, Bromley BR1 1QE
Tel: 020 8466 6139

The National Institute of Adult Continuing Education (NIACE)
Renaissance House, 20 Princess Road West, Leicester LE1 6TP
Telephone: 01162 044 200: Minicom: 01162 556 049

Fax: 01162 854 514
Email: enquiries@niace.org.uk

The Open University
Student Registration & Enquiry Service:
The Open University, PO Box 197, Milton Keynes MK7 6BJ

VOLUNTARY ORGANISATIONS

Should you wish to help others during your retirement you may like to contact the following:

The Volunteer Centre UK
Volunteer Centre Westminster, 53-55 Praed Street, London W2 1NR
Telephone: 020 7402 8076: Fax: 020 7402 3124
Email – info@volunteercentrewestminster.org.uk

Community Service Volunteers (CSV)
237, Pentonville Road
London N1 9NJ

Voluntary Service Overseas
Head Office, 317 Putney Bridge Road, London SW15 2PN
Telephone: 020 8780 7200

FINDING WORK

It is possible you would like to continue working. If so contact your local Job Centre or write to:

The British Chambers of Commerce
65 Petty France, London SW1H 9EU
Tel: 020 7654 5800: Fax: 020 7654 5819
Email: info@britishchambers.org.uk

Secrets Of Romany Long Life and Health

" . . . Their secrets are not so much a mystery but simply a way of life based on common sense …

- Avoid stress and strain always. Do not rush things but take your time and make perfection your goal, not the clock.
- Let tomorrow take care of tomorrow.
- Get plenty of fresh air whenever you can, as it has a magical effect on the body.
- Walk instead of riding around; use your body or it will get old and fat.
- As far as you can, rise with the sun and go to sleep with it; all nature does and so should you.
- Eat healthily by eating only fresh, simple, wholesome life-giving foods and avoid like the plague all stodgy, sickly, artificial, poor quality foods.
- Eat sparingly of rice, pasta and sweets but eat your fill of all manner of herbs, vegetables, fruit, buttermilk, malted milk, wholemeal bread and oats.
- Never cook in aluminium pots and pans but instead use ironware; aluminium impairs the quality of food and can cause symptoms in sensitive people.
- Never peel vegetables such as potatoes because the skin contains much goodness that keeps your skin and hair healthy. Never use onions that have been cut and left for a while as they draw germs into them (as with leaving cut onions in a newly painted room).
- Never discard outer leaves of vegetables, even if they are full of grub holes, for they contain more vitamins and nutrients than the paler inner leaves. Eat plenty of lettuce. It is a wonderful food, full of goodness . . ."

(Extract taken from *The Complete Country Bizarre – No's 1 – 11*. Originally published in 1970-74 and edited by Andy Pittaway and Bernard Scofield.)

Money
Solutions

Bill Habets

Notice To Readers

Although every effort has been made to ensure the accuracy of the information provided in this publication at time of going to press, neither the author nor the publishers can accept responsibility or liability for that information, this including any of the opinions or advice expressed in the following pages.

Chapter One

Why Problems With Debt
Are So Widespread

Debt has become an overwhelming problem in this country in recent years. While there have always been some people who had trouble either meeting their financial obligations or obtaining credit, the number of these has vastly increased within a short period of time. In fact, it has been estimated that there are probably twice as many people with severe money problems today than there were a decade ago.

Exactly why this has happened is not fully understood, although some of the major contributing factors are well known. According to personal finance experts, included amongst the major causes for the sudden explosion in credit – and accompanying debt burdens – are:

❑ The simple fact that the cost of borrowing is quite cheap at this moment, even though the Bank of England has recently ever so slightly increased the base rate for lending. Because borrowing is so inexpensive, people are more tempted to finance more and more items, rather than to pay cash for them.

❑ Expectations have gone up over the years. Not surprisingly, people want more and more of the better things in life, be it furniture for the home, a new car, gadgets and entertainment devices, or simply an altogether more luxurious lifestyle.

❑ Another major contributor to the expansion of credit has been the quite remarkable rise in house prices in recent years. After all, or so reason many, what is the point of putting money aside for an uncertain future when it seems that every week or so the value of your home is going up by perhaps as much as £1,000.

❑ One more important factor is the incredible pressure that retailers and finance organisations place upon the buying public, suggesting that they should buy now, because after all they will be given – 'given' being a word that is somewhat misused in this context – lengthy periods of interest-free credit. It's not uncommon for the more aggressive vendors, such as the multiples in the electronics, furniture, or kitchen replacement fields, to publish full-page ads in the national papers, saying 'nothing to pay for a whole year', conveniently forgetting to add that the interest charged after the initial period will be at a rate that would have made Scrooge blush!

However, while the background to the ever-rising tide of debt is intriguing, what really matters is the harm this has done to literally millions of ordinary people, dragging them into an ever increasing spiral of indebtedness and credit problems.

There are probably just as many different reasons for going into debt than there are people – and this means that there are good reasons, bad reasons, and so-so reasons. But, whatever may be the particular reason why you are having a problem with debt, it may or may not, be a consolation to you that your difficulties are not unique to you. In fact, if a recent advertisement from Compass Finance (this, admittedly, being an organisation with a stake in attracting borrowers) is to be believed you are in the same boat as about 15 million other people, who the ad says are 'currently blacklisted from obtaining credit', this representing about a quarter of the United Kingdom's population and nearly a third of the adult population.

Frightening though that statistic is, it is also somewhat misleading. Yes, there are probably some 15 million people who are likely to have difficulty in obtaining credit, but that does not mean that they are not worthy or deserving of credit. It simply means that, for one reason or another, they have fallen foul of the system by which creditworthiness is assessed.

Sadly, it only requires the slightest of financial 'misconduct' to end up on a blacklist. For example, in some instances, people have had their credit records besmirched simply because of being a few days late in making a hire purchase payment, or even been adjudged to be poor credit risks because in an effort to get the best deal possible they contacted several finance companies for quotations, and each of these companies reported the enquiry so that the total number of these suggested that the applicant was already having some difficulty in obtaining credit.

It is also worth pointing out at this point that one of the major contributors to the current difficulties faced by so many people is that the real cost of buying on credit is often less than obvious, and that many buyers only get into trouble because the interest charges they are paying are considerably higher then they had estimated or budgeted for.

Although lenders must now by law be totally truthful and accurate about the rate of interest they charge and how much this interest is going to add up to over the period of the transaction, it's only too easy for would-be borrowers – in their eagerness to acquire whatever their heart's desire may be set upon – to ignore these harsh realities of borrowing and only concern themselves with what the monthly repayments are going to be. And if these payments appear to be reasonably affordable, often little further thought may be given to the fact that the total cost of a purchase may well end up being as much as double the base price of the item bought.

Purchasers can also be misled into making commitment they can't quite afford because they are often likely to remain unaware of how much the total interest charged on their borrowing is adding to their final bill is because other items – such as insurance, maintenance contracts, extended guarantees, and delivery charges – are added to their account and interest then applied to the whole lot. As a result, purchasers easily deceive themselves into thinking that they're only paying interest on a given sum – that representing their basic purchase – but in reality they will also be paying interest on *all* the added extras.

The above are but a few of the reasons why people can only too quickly find themselves submerged under a mountain of debt, a mountain that keeps on growing and growing until it seems quite impossible to ever get out from under the accumulating pressure of unpaid bills. In such circumstances, it's obviously only too likely that some bills will either remain unpaid or be paid late ... with the net result that black marks will start to appear on the person's credit record, this almost certainly making them ineligible for further credit.

Another only too common reason for credit being refused is because an applicant is confused with someone else with the same or a similar name. Additionally, just living at an address previously occupied by someone with a bad credit record can be enough to make you also deemed, albeit wholly unjustly, unworthy of credit. Unworthy, that is, until you have the matter sorted out.

That last sentence, of course, hints at what is perhaps the most important underlying aspect of the next chapters: how to solve and deal with any credit problems you may encounter, and also how to ensure that these don't come up in the first place. Accordingly, in the pages that follow, you will find detailed and precise instructions on how to overcome all common problems associated with your personal credit worthiness as well as valuable general guidelines that will help you obtain any credit you may need at the best possible terms.

And to start at the beginning, the very first subject we will look at in the next chapter will be the various reasons why you may have difficulty obtaining credit – and what can be done to rectify the situation.

Chapter Two

Why You May Have Trouble Getting Credit

If you have been experiencing problem in obtaining credit of any sort – whether when applying for a charge card, a loan, a mortgage, hire purchase, or even when just wanting to rent a TV – the chances are high that your difficulties stem from one or two basic reasons.

The first of these – and the most likely in most cases – is that when the lender checked your credit history, information came to light that made him think of you as a bad risk – and this caused your application to be rejected.

However, even if your credit history checked out just fine, some of the information you supplied when you applied for credit wasn't found sufficiently satisfactory to meet the lender's own criteria for determining whether that particular line of credit should be granted.

This means that you can have trouble getting credit because either your credit record is flawed or because you and your circumstances simply don't match a particular lender's profile of the kind of clients he prefers. Naturally, it can also happen that you were turned down because a combination of *both* of these factors worked against you.

Of the two main reasons, the one most commonly responsible for a credit application being refused is a credit history that is considered unsatisfactory, and it is how to deal with this that is covered in depth in this and the next chapter (how to handle the other main reason for a refusal is covered in full in *Chapter 4*, which also explains the best way to apply for all kinds of credit so that you increase your chances of success, as well as providing information about lenders who are most likely to be receptive).

WHAT IS MEANT BY A CREDIT HISTORY?

The short answer to this question is that your credit history is made up of everything that's known about credit of any kind you've ever had – and, in some instances, not even actually had but merely had applied for.

As you might expect, one of the major factors that any lender will take into account when considering granting you credit is how well you've discharged your obligations in past transactions. Naturally, in many instances, the prospective lender may already be very well informed about at least part of your credit history, simply because you've had previous credit with him. Just as often, however, the lender may know precious little about you, other than what you've told him on your application form or during an interview. While that information will at least temporarily be accepted at face value, it will be also be subjected to a number of rigorous checks to ensure its veracity – and one of these key checks is for the lender to obtain a copy of your 'credit file'.

Let me explain exactly what 'credit file' means:

❑ A credit file consists of *all* and *any* available documents that contain information about your credit history or credit-worthiness, and as such there could be some kind of credit file about you held by anyone with whom you've had any financial dealings whatsoever.

❑ Much more commonly, however, the phrase 'credit file' refers to a specific set of documentation, or rather a computerised data base, in which are recorded various known facts about your credit.

The last mentioned type of credit files are compiled centrally by specialised agencies – called, as you might expect, credit reference agencies – who then sell this information to organisations wanting to check up on someone's credit history. Even if you've never been involved in any kind of credit transaction – or applied for credit – a credit file of that kind almost certainly exists about you, though the information recorded in it may be very limited indeed, perhaps consisting of no more than your name and address.

It is important to be aware that although credit reference agencies can and do supply information about your credit history, they do not operate what is generally known as a 'blacklist', that is a list of people whose record is so unsatisfactory that they should not be granted credit.

However what can and does happen is that factual but negative information about a borrower (such as having sought to defraud, regularly missed payments, having to be pursued through the courts, and so on) is transmitted by a lender to a credit reference agency and so ends up on the borrower's credit file. Damming though this information may be, the credit reference agency passes no judgment of any kind on it, but merely passes this information on to legitimate enquirers who are then left to reach to their own independent opinion as to whether that should stop *them* from offering credit.

It cannot be stressed too strongly that all lenders make their *own* decision, and that credit lapses that might cause you to be refused by one lender may well be considered to acceptable by another (especially one that specialises in taking on relatively poor credit risks, but charges accordingly high interest rates).

The extent to which your credit file can, for better or worse, affect any application you make for credit will, of course, depend greatly upon what kind of information it contains, whether this is mainly *positive* (that is, a record of properly maintained credit transactions) or *negative* (a list of obligations you failed to meet). A credit file is in many ways a double-edged sword: enough bad entries on it will cut you off from most, perhaps all, credit; lots of good entries will, however, often carry sufficient weight in themselves so this accumulated evidence of properly conducted previous transactions may then cut out some of the other stages that a credit application is usually put through.

The key point is that what your credit file says about you will almost certainly play a crucial role in any application you make for credit. It is therefore vitally important that this record is completely accurate – and, of course, also presents as favourable a picture as possible. How you can make sure that this is the case is now explained in full, beginning with how to find what your credit file has to say about you.

IF YOU WANT TO BE SURE IT'S DONE RIGHT, DO IT YOURSELF!

While credit reference agencies and the other organisations and businesses who supply them with information about you have a duty to make sure that this information is accurate and fair, errors can and do happen. There is *only one* absolutely certain way to ensure that each and every entry on your file is accurate, and that is to get a copy of it and check out every last detail yourself.

It is generally accepted that is a good idea for everyone to now and then check their credit file, but this becomes all the more important under certain circumstances, these typically including:

❑ You're about to apply for a substantial amount of credit. It follows that, the bigger the loan you're after, the more carefully your credit history will be checked, so you need to be sure that the record is absolutely correct.

❑ You have had some problems with credit in the past – perhaps missing the occasional payment, having charge accounts cancelled, even perhaps had a County Court judgments or two – and you want to find out whether these former lapses will still show up during a credit search (if they do, you can still usually take most, perhaps all, of the sting out of them, as is explained in the next chapter).

These are all excellent reasons why you should check your credit file, but another time when this is obviously imperative is when you've had an application for credit refused. While lenders do not have to tell you *exactly* why they refused you, they are obliged by law to give you a reasonable indication of why they did so.

One possible explanation for a refusal to grant credit is because your application may not have done well enough on the lender's *scoring system* (what this is and how it works is fully explained in *Chapter 4*). Even when a lender tells you that information from a credit reference agency played no part in their decision, they must still tell you, if requested by you to do so, whether they obtained information about you from an agency if the amount of credit involved was £15,000 or less.

Most lenders are usually quite forthcoming when asked why an application was turned down; others are often much less co-operative and may have to be persuaded into fulfilling their legal duty of informing you about any checks requested from credit reference agencies. To make such a close-mouthed lender own up, you can write to him (preferably by Recorded Delivery and within 28 days of the last time you were in contact with him about the proposed credit) along these lines:

> *Your name*
> *Your address*
> *Date*
> *Dear Anyloan Company:*
> *I refer to the recent application I made for a loan (your reference: XXX, XXX).*
> *As provided for under section 157 of the Consumer Credit Act 1974, I ask you to provide me with the name and address of any credit reference agency you have contacted to obtain information about me.*
> *As also provided for in the above Act, I expect to receive your reply within seven working days from the time you get this letter.*
> *Yours sincerely,*
> *Your name*

According to circumstances, the lender can respond to your letter in one of two ways:

1) If he *did* get information about you from a credit reference agency, he has a legal obligation to tell you which one/s he contacted; or

2) If he did *not* consult a credit information agency, he does not have to tell you he didn't. In fact, he's actually entitled to not bother replying to your letter at all.

CHECK OR NO CHECK – YOU STILL NEED TO FIND OUT

No matter whether a credit reference agency was contacted or not, you'll still want to find out what your credit file says about you because:

❑ If an agency was consulted, you need to find out what they said about you – just in case it was the information they provided that made the lender turn you down. Should there be negative entries in your file that can be corrected or rectified, the lender may want to reconsider his decision once these corrections are made.

❑ If an agency was not consulted, the fact that your application was turned down almost certainly means that you'll be applying elsewhere for credit, so it's worth making sure that your credit file is as clean as can be just in case the next lender you approach does consult a credit reference agency.

Of course, it is always considerably better to close the stable door before the horse has bolted, and it is equally preferable to check your credit file some time *before* you apply for credit – that way, you'll have time to sort out anything that needs attention before a prospective lender gets to see your file in its uncorrected version.

YOUR LEGAL RIGHT TO SEE A COPY OF YOUR CREDIT FILE

You have an absolute legal right to see a copy of what's held on file about you by a credit reference agency at any time, whether or not you've applied for or are planning to apply for credit.

Currently, there are three major credit reference agencies in this country that provide information about private individuals to their clients (other agencies, such as Dunn and Bradstreet deal with references about businesses). The agencies specialising in consumer credit records, listed here in alphabetical order together with their contact details, are:

❑ **Call Credit**,
Consumer Services Team, PO Box 491, Leeds LS3 1WZ,
Tel: 0870 060 1414; website: www.callcredit.plc.uk.

- **Equifax Europe (UK) Ltd,**
  Credit File Advice Centre, PO Box 1140, Bradford BD1 5US;
  Tel: 0870 010 0583; website: www.equifax.co.uk.

- **Experian Ltd,**
  Consumer Help Service,
  PO Box 8000, Nottingham NG1 5GX;
  Tel: 0870 241 6212; website: www.experian.co.uk.

These agencies are all well-established, and they take pride in doing their very best to not only ensure that their records are accurate but in also providing help to consumers when a problem does occur. Although the information an agency provides on your credit file will usually be broadly similar to that held by the other two, there can be differences because some of the information comes from the agency's own customers on a reciprocal basis – that is, that in order to be able to access the information, the client is also required to make similar data available to the agency.

This means that there is always is a distinct possibility that an entry may exist on one agency's file and not elsewhere. Accordingly, it really is best to get a copy of your credit file from *all three* agencies if you want to make absolutely sure of what a credit search could reveal. While, if you ask in time as explained above, a lender has to tell you afterwards whether he used a credit agency, and if so which one, he almost certainly is not going to tell this you beforehand – and that means that to be wholly certain that a search only finds properly recorded information, you really do have to get a copy of your file from all agencies. To obtain copies of your files, write separately to the agencies at the addresses given above along these lines:

Your name
Your address
Date
Dear credit reference agency:
> *In accordance with the provision made under section 158(1) of the Consumer Credit Act 1974, please send me a copy of my credit file. Enclosed please find a crossed*

cheque/postal order (remove that which doesn't apply) *for £2 made payable to yourselves.*

For your information, I have lived at the address mentioned above for the past seven (or whatever) *years.*

As provided for by the Act, I shall expect a reply from you within seven working days of the time you receive this letter. Yours faithfully,

Your name (as fully as possible, such as Alistair William Johnson).

If relevant to your circumstances, there is additional information you should also include because this will make it easier for the agency to track down any information in full (after all, making their lives easier is not so much a question of helping *them*, but of helping yourself).

Items to also include in your letter, if relevant, include:

❑ Should you have lived at your current address for less than six years, it can help if you also list your previous addresses and how long you lived there. For example:

I have lived at the address mentioned above for the past three years. Before that my addresses were (mention address in full) *from 1985 to 1987, and* (once again, mention address in full) *from 1987 to 2000.*

❑ If you are self-employed or in a partnership and use a trading name for your business, provide this information as well (but do not bother to do so if your business is a limited company, as these do not have any rights under the Consumer Credit Act. For example:

Apart from trading under my own name as a self-employed builder, I also trade in partnership with my wife, Wendy, of the same address, under the following two names: 'Apex Building Services' and 'Apex Roofing', both also of this address (state the business address/es, if these differ from your home).

❑ If your name has changed (a woman because she married, or anyone changing it legally by deed poll) within the past seven years, you should also mention this. For example:

Until my marriage three years ago, my surname was Jones; or: my name was changed by deed poll in March 1989; before that it was (state previous name in full).

Once you've posted your letter – there is generally no need to send it by recorded or registered post – it must be answered by the agency within seven working days after they receive it. If an answer fails to arrive on time, give the agency a couple of days' grace and if nothing has turned up then, write again, this time in the strongest possible terms to remind them of their legal obligations.

Usually, you will receive a reply within the deadline, and the agency's answer will be one of three things:

1. A copy of your credit file, this invariably accompanied by a standard covering letter and one or more helpful advice leaflets; or

2. A request from the agency asking for more detailed information about you because it's having some difficulty identifying you and/or tracing your file. Answer such a response without delay and tell them what they ask for in so far as you can do so (usually these enquiries seek clarification of addresses or names). Note that a new seven working days deadline starts from the time the agency gets your second letter.

3. A letter from the agency stating that they hold no information about you. Naturally, if there is no file, there's nothing you can do about something that doesn't exist – *unless, of course, a lender has told you that they had received information about you from that particular agency.* In the unlikely event of this happening, contact the agency again, asking them to sort out the discrepancy.

WHAT TO LOOK FOR IN YOUR CREDIT FILE

Once you've received your file, you then need to very carefully scrutinise each and every entry in detail to make sure that everything is exactly as it should be – as well as noting any items that may require clarification or 'repair' (full details of how to do this are provided in the next chapter).

Here, to help you identify items that may need attention, is a step-by-step guide that takes you through the various types of entries your file is likely to contain. As you work your way through this guide, there are four important points we should keep in mind:

1. Although credit files from the three agencies essentially contain the same kind of information, the way this information is presented – and the sequence it follows – can differ. Some of the examples that follow are based on a combination of these various forms of presentation.

2. To provide suitable examples, the hypothetical file we'll be looking at contains a combination of 'good' and 'bad' entries that is most unlikely to ever occur in real life. So don't be surprised if your file is a lot shorter and contains a great deal less information.

3. Names and addresses in the example file are all wholly fictitious and, as the phrase has it, any resemblance to real people is completely unintentional!

4. To make it absolutely clear what are credit file examples and what are comments about these entries, the examples are printed in bold characters similar to those produced by an ordinary typewriter – like this – and the comments appear in the same typeface as the rest of this book.

Let's now dissect our sample credit file section by section …

DETAILS FROM THE ELECTORAL ROLL

The first entry at your credit file will consist of information the agency will have obtained from the Electoral Roll and this will look somewhat like this:

ELECTORAL ROLL INFORMATION,
Local Authority ANYTOWN

```
AT 14 Anyroad, Anytown, Any County XX7 X20.
William Jones, 1988-2002
Patricia Jones, 1988-2002
Alexander Jones, 2000-2002
Sue Jones, 1997-2002
```

What that says is that the people named above are currently shown on the register of electors as living at that address. Additionally, it shows how long they've lived there – note, however, that people don't appear on the electoral roll until they're old enough to vote, so it is likely that Alexander and Sue are children who recently reached their majority.

Points to keep in mind when looking at this information:

❑ The reference agencies' electoral roll information only covers a limited period, usually from about 1980 or so. If a date is shown for when you left a previous address, that's not necessarily accurate because local authorities do not always update their electoral rolls at the same time. Although a slight error in dates is not likely to be relevant to credit-worthiness, it's worth letting the agency know the correct date.

❑ Names of the people who lived at your address before you moved there may also be shown. For example, the entry above could have an extra line that said: **Heather Wilson, 1982-2001.** An entry like that is not important, unless, of course, a previous resident is shown as still actually living at your address – in that case inform both the agency and the Electoral Roll Officer at your local council to have the entry brought up to date.

❑ Everyone who is eligible to vote and lives at your address will be shown, including tenants and relatives. The appearance of these people's name on your credit file is of no importance because the information in this section is wholly non-financial and therefore does not affect your personal credit-worthiness.

WHO HAS BEEN ASKING QUESTIONS ABOUT YOU?

Depending upon the kind of file you are looking at, this section may be called 'search information' or 'previous enquiries', and may be near the beginning or towards the end of the file. Whatever this section is called or wherever it is located, it reveals who has been asking questions about you as it provides a record of the enquiries the agency has had about you or members of your family.

This is what the entries, if any, will look like:

```
Mrs Pat Jones,
14 Anyroad, Anytown, Any County XX7 X20
Born 11/11/52.
At address: 10+ years
Searched on 06/08/99 by Anytown Credit Card
Company
Application type: CREDIT CARD - £2,000
Mr William A. Jones,
14 Anyroad, Anytown, Any County XX7 X20
Born 8/9/46
At address: 11+ years
Searched on 28/4/00 by Anytown Stockbrokers
Ltd
Search type: CREDIT ENQUIRY
```

This information is provided because it can help a prospective lender spot unusual credit activity that may suggest financial difficulties or even fraud. You can usually safely ignore entries in this section, unless, of course, a search took place by an organisation with which you have had no dealings. If that happens, contact them to find out why they asked for information about you. If you're not satisfied by their answer, contact both the credit reference agency and The Data Protection Registrar (see the *Appendix* for the address).

However, it is also useful to know that this record of previous enquiries is only maintained by the credit reference agencies for a limited period – one year by Experian; two years by Equifax and Callcredit. Equifax also uses a two-letter code to identify the kind of check carried out – the main ones are: AV, address verification check; LA, loss adjustment check; IB, insurance broker check; HI, health insurance check; LI, life insurance check; and DC, debt collector. The last-named is particularly relevant because it, by definition, suggests that you've come to the attention of a debt-collecting agency – something that is obviously bad news for anyone thinking of granting you credit!

WHAT ARE YOUR EXISTING CREDIT ARRANGEMENTS?

There will also be a section that lists known details of your current and past credit arrangements, and which will be called 'Insight Information' or 'Credit account information'. No matter its name, this is a vitally important part of your credit history because it reveals whether you've fallen in arrears or defaulted in some other way in previous credit arrangements.

The agencies present that information rather differently, and entries in this section will broadly resemble either of two following examples:

Example 1

```
        ANY TOWN MASTERCARD CREDIT
Mr W. A. Jones
Balances                    Limit      £5,500
                            Outstanding

    £120
                            Written off      £0
Effective dates             Start      11/06/94
                            Birth      08/09/46
Insight last updated                   25/09/03
Monthly status              000000000000
```

Example 2

The truly relevant part of this section – headed either 'monthly status' or 'status history' – is the series of numbers that indicates whether you're a prompt payer or not. Here is how you interpret that code:

❑ It consists of up to twelve numerals or letters, each one representing a month. If the account is current, the code will be a record of the past year; if the account is now closed, the code reflects what happened during its last 12 months.

❑ You read the code from left to right – the symbol at left being for

Mrs Patricia Jones,
14 Anyroad, Anytown, Any County XX7 X20
Anytown Credit Card Company,
CREDIT CARD/REVOLVING CREDIT
Started 03/06/93   Balance £647
                          Credit card limit £8,200
Status history   000000000000
In past 36 months, number of status 1-2 is 0; no
of status 3+ is 0
Details updated 24/07/03

the most recent month, the next symbol for the previous month, and so on.

❑   The symbols have the following meanings:

0 = payments are up to date.

1 = payments are up to one payment late.

2, 3, 4, 5 and 6 = payments are respectively two, three, four, five or six payments late.

8 or 9 = The account is in default. This means not only that the customer has failed to make payments on time but has also failed to respond satisfactorily to requests that the account be brought up to order.

D = account is either inactive or was dormant that month.

U = account status unclassified (this has neither a negative or positive meaning; it just means that for one reason or another, such as the customer querying a statement, the account's status does not fall neatly into any of the other categories.

Putting this in a nutshell, codes that are all or nearly all 0s, with perhaps only the occasional 1 or 2 will be accepted by most lenders as evidence of a 'good' payer; more than one 3 (especially if there are also lots of 2s) is seen as an indication of someone who may easily get into difficulty if they take on any more commitments; numbers higher than 4 sound a loud warning bell for potential lenders.

Points to note:

❑   Even though you've scrupulously honoured all your commitments on time, you may find that a 1 code still appears now and then on your record because, for example, your payment was delayed in the post.

❑ What kind of credit do you already have? Having lots and lots of credit accounts does not in itself make you a better credit bet – but if you have several and they're all in good order, that will usually be in your favour.

❑ How credit-worthy have other lenders judged you to be? Do you have high, low, or medium limits on your credit cards? How lenders who have dealt with you for some time judge your credit-worthiness will strongly influence a new lender.

❑ Are you already dangerously close to becoming over-committed? If you're using all of your credit limits to the full or nearly so, this may count against you, especially if a bit of simple arithmetic suggests to a new lender that you're already using all of your disposable income to meet existing commitments.

The entries described so far are those that might be expected to be found in the credit file of anyone who has credit transactions. Essentially what they do is confirm a borrower's identity, his place of residence, and give an encapsulated history of his credit dealings. However, credit files can also contain other information that can have a much greater impact upon someone's credit-worthiness and it is these we now look at.

THE POSSESSIONS REGISTER

The Possessions Register was established in August 1991 by the Council of Mortgage Lenders (CML), a national organisation whose membership includes all major mortgage lenders, in conjunction with the two major credit reference agencies to record details of borrowers whose properties have been taken into possession by a lender.

The prime purpose of this register is to prevent fraud, if a borrower were to attempt to obtain a mortgage without disclosing to a new lender that they had defaulted on a previous mortgage or had previously voluntarily surrendered their property.

The Register includes both cases where a borrower has voluntarily surrendered the property to the lender, as well as cases where possession was taken with a court order. The specific information held, and which would be shown on a credit file, includes:

- The name of the lender.
- The mortgage account number.
- The name of the borrower.
- The date of possession.
- The type of possession (whether by possession order or voluntary).
- Whether or not the outstanding debt has since been paid off or otherwise satisfied.
- The address of the property taken into possession.
- If known, both the previous and current addresses of the borrower.

All of the information held on the Register is submitted by the mortgage lender directly to the credit reference agencies.

The extent to which an entry in this register would affect later applications for credit does vary. Says the CML: 'Although past credit history would not necessarily preclude someone from obtaining another mortgage, it would naturally be taken into consideration by the lending institution. Where there is an outstanding debt, mortgage lenders will consider each mortgage application on its own individual merits at the time of application.'

Borrowers' details are kept on the Register for six years from the date the possession took place, after which time the details are then automatically removed from the file.

PUBLIC RECORD OR COURT INFORMATION

In this section are recorded any County Court Judgments (these more commonly known as CCJs), administration orders, bankruptcies, and voluntary arrangements.

Any entry in this section will play a major role in determining someone's credit-worthiness as it's obvious that an application for credit by someone who had previously defaulted sufficiently badly on another credit arrangement to have to be pursued through the court system is going to be treated with extreme caution indeed.

According to the credit reference agency, this information may be headed 'Public Record Information' or 'Court Information'. No matter how labelled, the information itself will have been supplied to the agency by Registry Trust, an independent organisation established by the Lord Chancellor's Department, which automatically receives details of relevant cases from local courts and then makes it available to the agencies.

Although the credit reference agencies present court information somewhat differently, the facts recorded in this section for each court case will be the same. Here is what a typical entry looks like (this example is based on an Equifax entry, but the other agencies' presentation is sufficiently similar so that there can be no confusion):

```
                    COURT INFORMATION
At: 14 Anyroad, Anytown,     Any County
Court Date:                  11/8/99
Case number:                 004561
Court name:                  Any County
Judgment value:              £247
Name:                        Mr William Jones
Satisfied:                   2/4/95
```

Normally, details of CCJs are kept on your credit file for six years from the date of the court case; they are automatically removed after that time. Note, however, that special conditions apply when a judgment is paid speedily:

- ❑ If the judgment is paid in less than a month, the record of it will be removed from the credit file.
- ❑ If the judgment is paid later than one month, the entry will not be removed but will be marked as 'Satisfied' – like the one shown in the example above.
- ❑ Until the debt is paid, the judgment will remain marked 'Unsatisfied'.

Other important points to note about any entries in this section:

❑ Apart from the obvious (were there indeed such CCJs? Are the amounts, dates, etc., shown correct?), make sure that any judgment that has been satisfied – that is, you've paid it fully – is shown as such. How to correct an error is explained in the next chapter.

❑ While the facts may be correct, do they fail to tell the full story as there may be mitigating factors that might put the whole episode in a somewhat different light and thereby alter a prospective lender's perception of it? See the next chapter about how you can present your side of the story in your credit file.

Apart from any individual CCJs, this section may also contain details of an Administration Order granted by a court. Here is a brief explanation of what these are:

❑ Anyone who has at least one judgment debt outstanding and whose total debts are less than £5,000 can ask the court for an administration order. If the court grants this, then all the outstanding debts will be, as it were, consolidated into one single big debt and the debtor repays this as agreed directly to the court, which in turn distributes the money it receives on a pro-rata basis to the various debtors.

One peculiarity of this system is that courts do not act uniformly throughout the country when deciding what debts are to be counted towards the £5,000 limit – some include the amount outstanding on a mortgage as part of this; others do not.

Under the Public Record Information or Court Information headings, you will also find details of any bankruptcies and voluntary arrangements, the later being a formal and supervised arrangement under which a debtor can stave off other legal proceedings by 'voluntarily arranging' with his creditors to pay off his debts in a mutually agreed way.

The information for these entries is obtained by the agencies from the official Gazettes and the Insolvency Service and the entries are held on file for six years. However, should a bankruptcy be annulled or discharged – or a voluntary arrangement completed – the record will then be amended.

This is what this sort of entry looks like:

```
Mrs Patricia Jones
Date 4/6/02
Information type: Voluntary Arrangement
Source: Department of Trade and Industry
```

As you can see from the example above, the details recorded are very scant and fail to the reveal the extent of the financial difficulties of the person named, other than that they were obviously sufficiently severe to result in bankruptcy or necessitate a voluntary arrangement, this usually, but not always, effectively putting an end to any applicant's quest for new credit.

WHERE ARE THEY NOW?

The credit reference agencies are members of the Gone Away Information Network (GAIN) through which lenders share information on clients with debts who appear to be have disappeared without trace.

Entries will appear in this section if all three of the following conditions are met:

1. The named individual is believed to be no longer resident at the stated address; and
2. The lender was not provided with or have a forwarding address for the borrower; and
3. A credit transaction was not fully up to date at the time the last known address became inoperative.

The information can consist of both the borrower's address at the time he originally took out the loan and any address to which he may subsequently have been traced. GAIN entries are retained on credit files for six years, the information they contain only being made available to other participating members of the network.

INFORMATION TO PREVENT FRAUD

The credit reference agencies also hold information provided by

The Credit Industry Fraud Avoidance System (CIFAS), a nationwide non-profit making organisation that was created in 1988 under the auspices of the Consumer Credit Trade Association, following concern at the increase in fraud, particularly against retail credit grantors, after the de-regulation of financial services.

The purpose of CIFAS is to prevent or limit fraud by the sharing of information between its members – which include all major lenders – about specific incidents of fraud and attempted fraud, the exchange of data taking place through the credit reference agencies.

Shown opposite is what a CIFAS entry might look like.

As seen in the last line above, the kind of fraud involved is usually shown, but sometimes this is only identified by a numerical code. Here's what these numbers, which are defined by CIFAS, stand for:

1 = 'Empty house' fraud – that is providing or using a false name and an existing address to fraudulently obtain credit.

2 = Impersonation – this defined as a fraudulent application for credit that involves the providing or using the name and particulars of another person.

3 = Successful 'massaging' of information to get credit – providing or using a genuine name and address but with one or more material falsehoods in personal details, or other relevant information to gain credit acceptance.

4 = Attempted fraud but which was spotted by the lender and the requested credit therefore not granted.

5 = The 'selling on' of assets to which the seller has no title. For example, the conversion (either by disposal or sale) of goods acquired under a hire purchase, conditional sale, contract hire, leasing or rental agreement, where ownership of the goods is vested in the grantor of the credit facility.

6 = Criminal 'first party' fraud of all types. For example, the opening of an account or other credit facility for the purpose of fraud, or the fraudulent misuse of an account.

Any potential lender will, of course, look extremely carefully at any CIFAS-originated entries for an address. If there is the slightest doubt

Credit Industry Fraud
Avoidance Scheme (CIFAS)

Information Registered

a)	Name used	Thomas Miscreant
b)	Address used	14 Anyroad,
		Anytown,
		Any County XX7 X20
c)	Date of information	22/10/96
d)	1. Credit grantors name and address	AnyTown Easy Credit Ltd (followed by address)
	2. Phone number	(number will be shown)
	3. Contact name	(a name will be shown)
	4. Case ref no	(a reference number will be shown)
e)	Type of case	IMPERSONATION OF ANOTHER PERSON

that an application for credit is genuine, the lender will contact the applicant to ensure that they had indeed applied for credit.

MISCELLANEOUS DATA

Any entry under this heading invariably is a 'Notice of Correction', consisting of text that you have asked the credit reference agency to add to your credit file to provide a fuller explanation for other entries that, although technically accurate, could be misleading because they fail to relate the full circumstances.

Such Notices of Correction are one of the most powerful tools you can use to 'clean up' a credit file. How and when to request the insertion of such a notice, as well as the many other perfectly legitimate ways through which you can improve your credit file, are covered in full in the next chapter.

Chapter Three

How To 'Repair' Or Improve Your Credit Record

Once you have obtained a copy of your credit file and gone through it in detail, as explained in the previous chapter, you will find find that the various entries in it fall in one of three categories:

1. Information that is wholly accurate and does not affect your credit-worthiness in any negative way. Obviously, there's no need to do anything in that case.

2. Information that although accurate in so far as it goes may possibly reflect negatively on your credit-worthiness. This kind of information is, of course, a candidate for the 'cleaning up' process that's fully explained in this chapter.

3. Information that is inaccurate, or at least is so in some respect. Whether or not any such inaccuracy is likely to affect your credit-worthiness, you should still have it amended or corrected.

Under the current Consumer Credit Act, you have several valuable legal rights if information in your credit file is wrong and could affect your credit-worthiness. Step-by-step instructions, together with sample letters, on how you make these rights work on your behalf are provided throughout this chapter, but first a quick look at what they are:

❑   If an entry is completely inaccurate, that is there is no basis for it at all, you can write to the credit reference agency and request that it removes the offending entry.

❑   If the entry is incorrect in some aspect (although there is some basis of fact for it) you can write to the agency and request that it either removes the entry or amends it. When writing, you should, of course, explain why you believe the entry to be incorrect and enclose copies of any documentation that supports your claim.

Here's a sample letter you can adapt as necessary when writing to a credit reference agency to have an entry removed or amended:

Your name
Your address
The date
Dear credit reference agency:
Thank you for sending me a copy of my credit file, your reference (quote reference number).
Unfortunately, the file contains an inaccuracy because…

…state in detail what the inaccurate entry is. For example: *'The second entry on page 3 states that I had a credit arrangement with the AnyTown Easy Loan Company – there was never any such loan and I've had no dealings whatsoever with that organisation';* or *'On page 5 the entry covering my credit record with the AnyTown Credit Card Company shows that I was apparently one month late with my payments on two occasions in the past twelve months – this is simply not so, as proven by the enclosed photocopies of my statements from them'.*

Once, you've explained what's wrong, then say what you want the agency to do about it…

Accordingly, I request that you delete that entry in its entirety (or 'amend it').

Please note that I'm writing under section 159(1) of the Consumer Credit Act 1974 and expect you to reply within 28 days of your receipt of this letter.
Yours faithfully,
Your name
Copies of documents enclosed: (list supporting documentation in full).

Once you've written to the agency as outlined above, it must reply within four weeks, telling you that it has done one of the following three things:

1. It has removed the entry from your file – as this is what you wanted to accomplish, there is nothing further for you to do, except perhaps to wait a couple of weeks and get a fresh copy of your credit file to make absolutely sure that the offending entry has really been removed and there was no slip-up along the way.

2. It has amended the entry. In that case, the agency must send you a copy of the amendment so you can study it to see if it fully meets your request. If the amendment is satisfactory, that once again is the end of the matter. If the amendment is not satisfactory, then see further below about what to do next.

3. It has taken no action. In other words, the agency decided that whatever you wrote failed to carry sufficient weight to make them alter or remove the offending entry because they believe it's accurate, despite your request.

Should the agency either produce an amendment that's unsatisfactory to you or tells you it has done nothing (or, as is much less likely to happen, fails to reply to your letter within the four-week deadline), you can then write once again, this time requesting that the agency adds a note – called a *Notice of Correction* – to your file to provide extra information about the entry in question and that a copy of this note must be included with information it supplic. .Jout you that's based on the entry in question.

Key points about drafting a Notice of Correction:

❑ This notice should provide a clear and accurate explanation of why you believe the entry to be incorrect or misleading.

❑ It must not be longer than 200 words.

❑ If the credit reference agency replied to your first letter – the one in which you objected to the entry – your Notice of Correction must be sent within four weeks of the date you received the agency's reply. But if the agency failed to reply to your letter within four weeks, your Notice of Correction must be sent to them within the next four weeks.

❑ If the agency accepts your Notice of Correction – that is, it agrees to your request that it should now form part of your credit file, it must tell you so within four weeks of receiving it.

To have a Notice of Correction placed in your file, write to the credit reference along these lines, adapting this as necessary:

Your name
Your address
Your phone number
The date
Dear credit reference company:
   Thank you for letter of (state date) *about my credit file* (state reference).
   I'm sorry to note that you refuse to remove (or: 'amend') *the entry I wrote to you about on* (state date).
   Accordingly, please add the following Notice of Correction to my file:

NOTICE OF CORRECTION

   I, William A. Jones, of 14 Anyroad, Anytown, Any County, XXX XXX, would like it to be known that...

...exactly what you write after the above will, of course, depend upon the point at issue. Here are some examples to help you choose your own words:

   '...the late payments recorded on my file in regards to the AnyTown Easy Credit Company only arose because their collector failed to turn up on two separate occasions as had been previously arranged.' Or:

   '...the arrears notified by the Anytown Car Loan Company arose because there was a dispute about the vehicle that had been bought with this loan and I withheld payments as a way to force them to come to an amicable and fair agreement. The dispute has now been settled and the payments are once again being made as agreed.' Or:

   '...although my credit file shows that I unfortunately had some difficulties in meeting my commitments in the early part of last year, this was because I was in hospital for several

weeks at that time following a serious operation. I have now fully recovered, am once again in full-time work, and am meeting all my credit commitments.'

Whatever may be the explanation you present in your Notice of Correction, it's a good idea to complete it with a sentence along these lines:

I would like anyone searching my credit file to take these facts into account.

I expect you to confirm within 28 days of your receiving this letter that you have added the above Notice of Correction to my credit file.

Yours faithfully,

Your name

If your Notice of Correction is accepted, that then is the end of the matter as far as you are concerned because any negative connotation that the original entry may have created will have been cleaned up as far as possible by the additional information that's now an integral part of your file.

While you will have done your part of the job, there are certain further things the credit reference agency must do if it agrees to either amend your file or adds your Notice of Correction to it:

❑ To begin with, the agency must send the revised details to any lender who searched your credit file during the six months preceding your original request for a copy of your file. This is done so that a lender who recently turned you may now perhaps change his mind because of the extra information.

❑ The new, revised information must be used on all future occasions.

❑ If your Notice of Correction relates to a County Court Judgment of a Sheriff Court Decree (more about these later), the Agency must also pass the new information on to Registry Trust Ltd, the official keeper of the Register of County Court Judgments. This organisation will in turn pass the information on to the other credit reference agencies so that your Notice of Correction will be automatically added to their credit file about you.

Things can, however, become a little bit more complicated if the agency rejects your Notice of Correction – it can do so because it considers it incorrect, defamatory, frivolous, scandalous, or unsuitable for some other reasons when that happens, the agency must refer the matter to the Information Commissioner for a final decision. The following events then take place:

❑ Within 24 working days of getting a request from an agency requesting his intervention, the Information Commissioner will contact you to get your comments on the matter.

❑ Based on such additional comments you may then supply as well as the agency's original request, the Information Commissioner will then make a decision to resolve the dispute, this decision having to be implemented by the agency if he says that your Notice of Correction (albeit possibly in a slightly altered form) must be added to your credit file.

The above, of course, is based on the sequence of events that occur if the agency – as it should – does contact the Information Commissioner because it believes your Notice of Correction unsuitable or unacceptable.

It can happen, however, that after having sent in your Notice of Correction, you just don't hear anything from the credit reference agency within 28 days, leaving you unaware of whether it has accepted it, rejected it, or contacted the Information Commissioner for a ruling.

In that case, you then directly approach the Information Commissioner yourself, writing him a letter along these lines

Your name
Your address
Your phone number
The date

The Information Commissioner,
Wycliffe House,
Wilmslow, Cheshire SK9 5AF.

Dear Information Commissioner:

I am writing under section 159 (5) of the Consumer Credit Act.

I recently obtained a copy of my credit file (quote its reference number) *from the Anytown Credit Reference Agency* (give full name and address of the agency).

Upon examining the file, I wrote to the agency on (state date) *and asked it to* ... (state exactly what you asked, whether it was to remove an entry, amend one, or to add a Notice of Correction).

It is now more than 28 days since I wrote to the agency and I have heard nothing from them.

It is my belief that if ... (re-state the remedy you sought, such as 'the amendment is not made' or 'the Notice of Correction is not added to my credit file') ... *this will be detrimental to my credit status.*

In view of the above, I'd appreciate it if you were to contact the credit reference agency on my behalf and seek to resolve the matter.

For your information, I enclose copies of all my letters to the agency.

Yours faithfully,

Your name

The copies of letters enclosed herewith are: (list these in detail).

Once your letter has been received by the Information Commissioner, the following will happen:

- ❑ He will within 14 working days ask the credit agency for its comments.
- ❑ A copy of the agency's reply to the Information Commissioner will also be sent to you, inviting any further comments from you.
- ❑ Once he has fully considered the views of both sides, the Information Commissioner will within two months of getting

information from both parties decide how the matter should be resolved, his decision being binding.

DEALING WITH PUBLIC RECORD AND COURT INFORMATION

As explained in the previous chapter, under this heading in your credit file will be found details of County Court judgments (hereafter referred to as CCJs), administration orders, bankruptcies and voluntary arrangements. More than other kind of negative information, apart of those suggesting fraud, any entries in this part of your file demand to be cleaned up as far as possible. Here's how you do that, starting with…

COUNTY COURT JUDGMENTS

If after a case in a county court a judgment is entered against you, the details of that judgment will generally be 'registered' on the Register of County Court Judgments. The record of these judgments will then eventually appear on your credit file, having been passed on to them by Registry Trust Ltd, the organisation that maintains the Register.

This is how you go about cleaning up that part of your file as far as possible…

❑ Even if you have a CCJ registered against you, if you pay the full amount of it within one month of the judgment date, you can ask the court to remove your name from the Register. You will have to pay a £3 fee for this and the court will give you a certificate to prove that you paid the CCJ within a month. On the basis of that certificate, you can contact the credit reference agencies to have the CCJ entry removed from your file (at times, this will have been done automatically, but it's best to make sure).

❑ Should it already be too late for the above remedy, the next best thing is to have the CCJ marked as 'satisfied', this meaning that you've paid it off. When first registered, unpaid CCJs are shown as 'unsatisfied' and a CCJ marked this way is really going to badly affect your chance for any future credit. On the other hand, someone who has 'satisfied' any CCJs will not suffer too badly under the scoring system used by many lenders and will probably be able to get most forms of credit if the rest of his record is pretty good.

To change an 'unsatisfied' CCJ entry into one that's marked 'satisfied', send the court where your case was heard a letter along these lines...

> *Your name*
> *Your address*
> *Your phone number*
> *The date*
>
> *The Anytown County Court,*
> *Anyroad,*
> *Anytown.*
>
> *Dear Sirs:*
> *I refer to the following County Court Judgment: case number XXX XXX William A. Jones (indicate both the case number and your full name).*
> *Enclosed herewith please find confirmation that this debt has now been paid in full: receipt from Anytown Tiling Company, dated 12/8/02 and marked 'Paid in full'.*
> *Accordingly, I'd appreciate it you were to have this judgment marked as 'Satisfied'.*
> *Also please find enclosed a cheque/postal order for £3 fee, this made payable to 'HM Paymaster General'.*
> *Yours sincerely,*
> *Your name*

When preparing a letter like the above, note that a £3 fee is to be paid for *each* case you want to have marked 'satisfied'.

Soon after writing, you should receive confirmation that the judgment is now marked as 'satisfied', this information then being passed on from the court via Registry Trust Ltd to the credit reference agencies. Once again, you may want to check on this by getting a new copy of your file from the agencies, but allow a few weeks to go by before you do this because it can take that long for records to be updated.

A variation on the above can happen when you've paid your judgment in full, but your former creditor for one reason or another refuses to give you written confirmation of this.

In that case, write to the court along the lines indicated above, except that the second paragraph in the main body of the letter should now say something this:

'I've now paid this amount in full to Anytown Tiling, but they have so far failed to send me the receipt they had promised',

... or whatever the case may be.

The court staff will now check the court's records; these may already show that you've paid in which case confirmation that your judgment has been marked 'satisfied' will be sent to you.

Should the payment not show up on the court records, the staff will then write to the person to whom you had owed the money. Either when your former creditor confirms payment – or if a month goes by without a reply to the court's letter – the judgment will be marked as 'satisfied'.

Finally, if you want to have an administration order (that's an arrangement by which various CCJs are lumped together into one big debt) shown as 'satisfied', once again write to the court and ask that they issue you with a certificate of satisfaction. You'll have to pay a £3 fee for this, but won't have to supply any receipts because you will, of course, have made the payment to the court and its records will show that the total debt has been paid in full.

The above shows you how to deal with CCJs in England and Wales. Things are slightly different in other parts of the UK:

❑ Scottish courts do not issue certificates to prove that you've paid your decree (the Scottish equivalent of a CCJ). If you've fully paid off a Scottish decree, you should write to the Registry Trust Ltd,

172/175 Cleveland Street, London, W1P 5PE, and enclose a receipt or letter of confirmation from the *pursuer;* that's what your creditor is called North of the border. This will then result in the entry being marked 'satisfied'.

❑ In Northern Ireland, send your receipt or other proof of payment to the *Enforcement of Judgments Office, 7th Floor, Bedford House, Belfast House BT2 7DS.* Any documentation that the Office issues in response should then be sent by you to the credit reference agencies so they can update their records.

Following the procedures outlined above will ensure that any CCJs that should not be on your file are removed, and that those you've paid are marked as 'satisfied', but there is one more thing you can do in the latter case and that is to offer an explanation as to why a CCJ came about in the first instance. You do this by asking the credit reference agency to add a Notice of Correction to your file, writing to them along the lines of the sample letter reproduced earlier in this chapter.

Just what you say in the explanation part of your notice will, of course, depend on what really happened, but statements like the following can greatly help reduce the negative effect of a CCJ:

A)   *I fell into arrears with my payments on this loan when I was made redundant from the job where I had worked for 17 years and it took me nearly a year to find new employment. Within two months of starting work again, I was able to pay off this debt in full.*

B)   *The CCJ arose because I was in dispute with the creditor because of a defect in the goods he supplied. When he at first refused to put matters right, I stopped my payments to force him to do something. By the time he sorted things out, the outstanding payments had accumulated to such an extent that I wasn't able to pay them off all at once and the supplier chose to take me to court rather than give me a little bit of extra time to pay him.*

The above are, of course, only examples but no matter what are the mitigating circumstances about a CCJ, it's worth having these included in your credit file as that can at times make all the difference to how a lender assesses your credit record.

BANKRUPTCIES AND VOLUNTARY ARRANGEMENTS

Other entries in the public record and court information section of your file that are potentially extremely damaging to your credit standing are those relating to bankruptcies and voluntary arrangements. While you cannot have these entries removed, do make sure that they carry as little sting as possible by having them amended as follows:

❑ If you were once declared bankrupt and the bankruptcy is now discharged or annulled, contact the Official Receiver who originally dealt with your case and ask for documentary evidence of the annulment or discharge.

❑ If you had previously entered into a voluntary arrangement and this was satisfactorily completed , ask the supervisor of the individual arrangement for documentary proof of the completion.

In either case, send the proof you received of discharge, annulment or completion to the credit reference agencies and ask them to amend your credit file accordingly.

OTHER PEOPLE'S CREDIT PROBLEMS MAY AFFECT YOURS

Part of your credit file may list other people living at your address. For example, you may find that previous occupiers of your home may also be shown in your file (they don't matter as there should be a date indicating when they left), as well as other members of your household. The inclusion of names of family members will generally have no effect upon your credit-worthiness as long as these people themselves either have a clean credit history or none (as is, of course, often the case with young adults).

However, should one or more members of your family have a bad credit history, this can certainly affect your credit-worthiness. For example, lenders may take into account a spouse's – or even a son's or daughter's – credit record when considering an application. This means that you could be refused credit simply because your son, who still lives at your home, has been a bad payer, even though your financial affairs are totally unconnected.

To deal with that kind of situation, you first of all need to be aware that, the agencies are restricted by law as to what *financial* information they can provide to lenders on the basis of name and address and this can be summed up as follows:

❑ Financial information may be provided about you; people who have the same name, or one that's very similar, and live at your address; members of your family living at the same address; people with the same name, or a very similar one, who have previously lived with you at either your current or a past address; and also other people who have previously lived with you as part of your family at either your current or past address.

❑ Agencies must not, however, when reporting your details, provide financial information about anyone in the following categories: people who have not lived at your current or last address as a member of your family at the same time you lived there; people about whom the agencies have information which makes it reasonable for them to be believe that you have no financial connection with them.

❑ Note that the restrictions above refer to financial information – agencies are entitled to, as they often do, supply the *names* of other people (whether or not these are members of your family) who are currently or were previously listed on the electoral roll for your address.

This is what to do to make certain that someone else's bad credit record does not affect your good one:

❑ Ensure that your credit record does not list anyone who is already excluded by virtue of the restrictions above.

❑ Even though other entries may fall within the guidelines they may still contain financial information about one or more other members of your family with whom you have no financial links. If that's the case, tell the agency that there's no financial connection, because it must then stop supplying financial information about these people when answering enquiries about you.

To set up a 'disassociation' – that's the technical term used by the credit industry – between you and other people in your family, all you have to do is write to the agency. Here's a sample letter you can adapt as required:

> *Your name*
> *Your address*
> *Your phone number*
> *The date*
> *Dear credit reference agency:*
> *Thank you for sending me a copy of my credit file.*
> *I note that this contains financial information about my son, Alexander Jones, who lives at this address. Although he lives at the same address as I do, he runs a separate household and there is no longer any financial connection between us.*
> *Accordingly, please create a disassociation between us, with the effect that financial information about him will no longer appear on my credit file, and, equally, that information about me will not appear on his credit file. I would appreciate it greatly if you were to confirm in writing to me that you have created this disassociation.*
> *Yours faithfully,*
> *Your name*

By the way, if *one* of the credit reference agencies accedes to your request for a disassociation, there's no need to also ask the other ones to do the same as this happens automatically because disassociation information is shared between all the agencies.

OTHER POSSIBLE ERRORS OR DISCREPANCIES

Apart from the above, there can be other erroneous or misleading statements on your file that do not neatly match any of the foregoing remedies.

If you have a problem of that kind – let's say, information supplied by a credit company shows you in arrears when you know you weren't – it can be best to approach the *supplier* of the information first rather than the credit reference agency.

Should the information supplier agree that the information they supplied was erroneous (mistakes can and do happen!), then get them to confirm in writing to you that they will have the entry altered or removed. Send a copy of that letter to the credit reference agency and ask them to confirm that they have indeed heard from information supplier and made the necessary correction.

Although this chapter has shown you exactly how to deal with every one of the main likely problems that may appear on your credit file, there's always a chance that you may encounter something that hasn't been dealt with specifically. Here's what to do in that unlikely event:

1. Write to the credit reference agency, explaining what the problem is and ask them to help you sort out the matter

2. Also write to the information provider, as all responsible companies and organisations will usually do their level best to sort out something that's gone wrong.

THE WORST KIND OF CREDIT HISTORY IS NOT TO HAVE ANY

Everything we've looked at so far in this chapter has been concerned with cleaning up an indifferent credit record to improve your chances of obtaining credit.

However, apart from people who have a poor credit history, there is another group of people who can have great difficulty in obtaining any kind of credit. Their problems, however, are not the result of a chequered credit history but are caused instead because they don't have one at all, it being one of the peculiarities of the way credit-worthiness is generally assessed that it can be just as damning not to have any kind of credit history as it is to have one that's less than perfect.

Not having a traceable credit history can cut you off from many forms of credit simply because most lenders, when deprived of the hard facts provided by credit files, then find it difficult to make a decision about someone who is essentially an unknown quantity.

Of course, the solution to this lies in establishing a credit record, so that potential lenders can find the documentary reassurance they need. But creating a credit history from scratch can be somewhat like trying to answer the old conundrum about what comes first: the chicken or the egg? If the chicken is a credit record, then how do you create this if you can't get credit? And if the egg is the credit you can only get if you've already got the chicken represented by an acceptable credit record, then how do you solve this paradoxical dilemma?

In fact, there are several ways around this seemingly insoluble problem – which one of these will work best for you will, of course, depend on your particular circumstances. Here are some ideas to consider:

❑ Open a bank account. You don't need a credit record to do this, although you will be asked to supply references. No matter how low the level of transactions in your account may be, keep it in good order and within a few months at the most the existence of a well-maintained bank account will become a key that unlocks your access to a successful application for a credit charge card. Operate your card account properly for a while and the entry this creates on your credit file will in turn open the way to other forms of credit.

❑ Should you experience difficulty opening a bank account, try a building society instead. Get a current account rather than a deposit one, even though you'll get less interest that way, because a current account generally brings with it an agreed overdraft limit. Though this overdraft will be for a very small amount – maybe as little as £250 – it is a form of credit and as such will be recorded on your credit file. Should the building society not want to give you a current account immediately, go for the deposit one, wait a little while (a couple of months or so) and then ask to have it altered to a current account.

❑ An easy to obtain form of credit are 'in-store' credit cards or hire purchase arrangements offered by major retail chains, the reason for this being that they want to sell you their merchandise. The next time you buy a reasonably expensive item – TV, video recorder, whatever – ask for finance and the chances are that you'll get it even without an established record. Once again, this first credit account will open the way to other types of credit.

❑ Even more likely to grant credit to an unknown quantity (although the amount involved will usually be very small) are the various home shopping catalogues, such as Grattan's or Littlewoods. Buy a set of saucepans on payments and this will automatically create that all-important first favourable entry on your credit file.

DON'T BE TEMPTED BY 'CREDIT REPAIR' PROMISES

There is one more aspect of credit repair that needs to be mentioned – and that's the so-called credit repair agencies whose enticing advertisements appear in many publications.

Usually, these agencies try to sell themselves to you by playing deliberately on your fears of what a poor credit history can mean to you and your family – and then offer to 'put in the fix' for a sizeable fee, this ranging from £100 to several times as much.

While it's true – as has been demonstrated several times in this chapter – that a great deal can be done to clean up a poor credit record, what can be achieved is limited both by legislation as well as by the practices of the various organisations that provide the various bits of information that together make up your credit file. What's more – once again, as shown in this book – every possible measure that can improve your credit file can be put into effect by your own efforts and there's no need to pay someone else to do this for you.

If despite the above, you're still tempted to use a repair agency, consider what Equifax, one of the main credit reference agencies that actually maintains and updates credit files, has to say about them: 'These agencies advertise that they are able to have personal County Court judgments and default records removed from the files of credit reference agencies – often for a substantial fee. However, County Court judgments can only be removed under certain specific circumstances, in which case, the procedures for doing so are quite simple, and do not require the services of a credit repair agency.'

More or less similar views about credit repair agencies have been expressed by The Office of Fair Trading. And if that isn't enough for you, then note these words from a leaflet by the Court Service, an executive agency of the Lord Chancellor's Department that amongst other things is charged with overseeing the County Courts system: 'It is not illegal to help someone with genuine reasons to have a judgment cancelled or removed. But court procedures are relatively straightforward and can normally be dealt with easily and cheaply without the help of a credit repair agency.'

Incidentally, be aware that if you are thinking about using an agency because you have a handicap that makes it difficult for you to write the necessary letters, you can usually get help with this absolutely for free by getting in touch with your local Citizens' Advice Bureau – see your local phone book for the address of your nearest branch.

PUTTING IT IN A NUTSHELL

Even the poorest of credit records can either be cleaned up to a great extent or at the very least presented in a better light. Either way, this will probably mean that a credit file that previously suggested too high a risk for most lenders will now stand a good chance of being considered acceptable.

However, to make sure that you get all the credit you want, you not only have to present the best possible credit record but you must also choose your prospective lender carefully as well as make your application in specific ways that will enhance your chances of success. Exactly how you do this is explained in full in the next chapter.

Chapter Four

How To Get The Loans And Credit You Want

Taking the steps outlined in the previous chapter will make an immense difference to how good your credit record looks to a prospective lender. But there will always be some instances where, despite your best 'clean-up' efforts, your record may still reveal some aspects of your past history that may count against you. Even in that situation, there are still many simple ways through which you can drastically increase your chances of success when applying for any kind of loan.

Just having a couple of black marks on your credit record does not exclude you from all, or even most, forms of credit. Usually, it just means you may have to work a little harder to get your application accepted, either by choosing your lender more carefully or by presenting your case in its very best light, or by a combination of these two methods.

To illustrate this, let us begin by looking broadly at the different stages that an application for credit – whether it's for an overdraft, a loan, a credit card, or whatever – usually has to go through:

1. Invariably, the starting point is a written application completed by you (although if you're applying during a meeting with a representative of the lender, he or she may actually fill in the form, leaving you just to sign it).

2. Most commonly, no decision will be made immediately. The reason why no immediate decision is made is because your application will be assessed by some form of 'credit scoring', this being a method that allocates various points to everything that's known about you and then adds these up to establish whether you score high enough to be offered the particular type of credit you're seeking.

3. Some time later, the lender will let you know what has been decided. If the answer is yes, then you won't be too interested in knowing what led up to it, but if it's a no, then you may be able to yet reverse this in one of several ways that are described later in this chapter.

We'll now look at these three steps in greater detail and see what you can do at the various stages to increase your chances of obtaining credit.

FILLING IN THE APPLICATION FORM

Two very important points about applying for any kind of credit:

❑ It should not be necessary to say this, but said it will be nevertheless: never deliberately falsify information in any way when you're applying for credit. Not only could this lead to a criminal prosecution under certain circumstances, but it will certainly cause your application to be rejected if you're caught out – as almost certainly you will be.

❑ Although you should never provide false information, you are, however, totally entitled to present yourself and your case in the best possible light, providing you do this in a totally honest manner.

To help you put the last thought into practice, these tips will help you fill in a credit application so that your good points are emphasised and the effect of any not-so-good ones are minimised:

❑ If you think it helpful to the case you're making, you need to expand your answers to do more than just baldly answer a question in the box provided. For example, if you've only lived at your current address and/or the immediately previous one for a short period of time, and you feel an explanation will help your application, then explain the reasons, such as:

The reason I moved so often was because promotion at work required frequent relocation.

If the space provided for your answer is too small for your longer answer, write it on the side of the form and link it to the box with an arrow.

❑ Another typical question that may be worth answering more fully is the one that asks how long you've been with your current employer. If you've only been working there a fairly short time, but had been with your previous employer for many years, say so:

Although I only recently joined this firm, immediately before that I worked for GoodCraft Jewellers for 14 years.

❑ Also follow this principle when filling in the boxes about your bank and building society if the accounts you have now have only been opened recently. For example:

Before switching my account to Barclays, I had previously banked with the Halifax (sort code: XX XX XX; Account no: XXXXXXX).

❑ Naturally, you'll be asked about your income and your answer deserves thinking about as the more money you have coming in, the more creditworthy you're likely to be considered. Therefore, be sure to take into account *all* your income, not just basic salary or wages, but also overtime, bonuses, interest on investments, rents received, earnings from occasional or part-time work, and even state benefits, such as children's allowance or whatever.

❑ Most application forms will also want to know about your outgoings. Don't rush to mention expenses that are 'one offs' or are wholly discretionary and to which you can easily put a stop. For example, while mortgage repayments and community charge are unavoidable long-term commitments, a subscription to pay-as-you-view television isn't, because you can cancel it if money becomes tight.

❑ Some might think that having dependent children is an indicator of stability; however, they are also by definition a financial commitment. For that reason make sure that you don't show as dependants children who although still living at home are themselves in employment and paying their own way by contributing to household expenses.

❑ If you are self-employed, think carefully how you describe your occupation if it genuinely fits more than one category. For example, someone who plays in a band but also teaches music would probably benefit from calling himself a teacher instead of a musician; and a marketing representative may appear a safer bet than a door-to-door salesman.

❑ When asking for a loan (as compared to applying for a credit card), you'll be asked to indicate what you plan to spend the money on, typically being offered boxes to tick under headings like home improvement, car purchase, general spending, holiday, or debt consolidation. If you can, without stretching the truth, tick 'home improvement', as that's likely to enhance your chances. Spending on home improvement is generally seen as a 'responsible' thing to do, but needing 'debt consolidation' obviously suggests that your financial affairs are less than straightforward.

❑ When applying for credit during an interview, remember that while whoever you're talking to may not be able to *approve* your loan (that decision is usually taken later), he or she can almost certainly influence your chances for better or worse according to the impression you create. Therefore be punctual, dress in a neat, clean and non-eyebrow raising manner, and bring with you whatever documentation supports your application.

❑ If you are self-employed, also bring copies of your accounts for the last three years and, if the size of your business warrants you having one, your business plan.

Another thing to consider, whether you apply by post or during an interview, is that you can take some of the sting out of negative information about you that the lender is bound to discover eventually by deliberately revealing it yourself. For example, if you've had a County Court judgment (something that is bound to come to light), say so up front and the lender may give this unfavourable factor less weight than if he thinks you had tried to hide it. If applying by post, think about writing a letter along these lines:

Dear Sirs:

Please find herewith my completed application for a loan for £2,000.

In all fairness, I feel I should mention that I've had a problem with a previous loan. What happened is that I was temporarily unemployed and unable to meet all the payments on time.

However, I am now in steady employment and the previous loan has been fully paid.

I hope that this previous lapse will not stop you from approving my current application.

Writing such a letter, altering the particulars to fit the circumstances, can bring you one of two benefits:

1. The lender may take your candid approach into account, perhaps literally giving you credit for being honest with him; or

2. If your lapse was such that this particular lender would not consider you because of it, he may just say no without bothering to check your credit record. The advantage of this is that if you're going to be turned down in any case, then it's better than this happens without your credit being checked because every such check is also noted on your credit file and too many checks can in themselves suggest poor credit worthiness to another lender.

THE LOW-DOWN ON CREDIT SCORING

Whilst the way in which you apply for credit can greatly influence the outcome, there is little you can do to affect the next stage. This stage is the one that is carried out behind the scenes in the lender's office when your application is reviewed and considered. Despite that, it's still useful to have an insight into this process because that knowledge can help you prepare your application so that, without any falsification whatever, it presents you and your request in the best possible light.

When assessing an application, lenders will usually take three main types of information into account when considering your suitability for credit. These are:

1. Information contained in the application itself.

2. What the borrower's credit reference file has to say about him or her.

3. What additional information was obtained during an interview, if there was one.

All this information is then 'credit scored'. There are many different systems of credit scoring but all work in essentially the same way: they allocate points to various facts about the applicant and it is the sum total of these points that determines whether credit will be granted and in what amount.

It is important to be aware that a given set of information will not always lead to the same conclusion when the points are totalled up. There are two main reasons for this:

1. Although the underlying principle is the same for all credit scoring systems, the number of points allocated to given factors isn't and can vary greatly from system to system; and

2. How well you have to score before getting credit also varies greatly between different lenders and organisations. For example, even when *exactly* the same scoring system is used by two different lenders (and that's unlikely), a score of, let's say, 80 may mean a refusal from one and acceptance by the other. The reason for this is that every lender has his own unique view about what he considers to be an acceptable risk.

Scoring systems are usually divided in several sections, some of which are not used when not relevant to a particular decision. Here is how a typical scoring system might be applied:

❑   The first section will invariably relate to your housing situation and points may be typically allocated as follows:

- ◆   You own or are buying the property in which you live: plus 20 points.

- ◆   You're renting an unfurnished home: plus 10 points. An extra 5 points may be added if your landlord is a council or a housing association; alternatively, 5 points may be deducted if you're renting from a private landlord.

- ◆   You're still living with your parents: plus 10 points.

- ◆ You've lived at the current address for more than three years: plus 20 points.
- ◆ You've changed addresses more than three times in the past three years: minus 10 points.
- ◆ You have a telephone account in your name: plus 5 points. Plus points – usually five of them – may also be given for having electricity, water, and gas accounts in your name.

❑ Next, points will be allocated according to what's known about you as a person:

- ◆ Your marital status: most commonly, you get some plus points for being married, while single people score either 10 minus points or none.
- ◆ Your age: generally, you'll get 20 plus points if you're older than 35 years of age; 10 plus points if aged between 27 and 35; and none if you're younger than 27. Very young applicants may also score minus points.
- ◆ Your occupation: most lenders give preference to people they think of as being in reliable and/or stable jobs, such as civil servants, council employees, teachers, professionals, health service workers, and so on. Belonging to one of these groups can bring an extra 10 to 20 plus points. Being in an occupation that, rightly or wrongly, is perceived as offering less stable employment, such as being a waiter or a bricklayer, may bring 5 or 10 minus points.
- ◆ How long you've been in your current job: the longer you've worked for the same employer, the more plus points you get, these usually being allocated on a sliding scale, such as 5 plus points for five years; 10 points for ten years; and so on.

❑ Additionally, what's known about your previous credit history will have a major effect upon how well you score. Typically, points may be allocated as follows:

- ◆ Having no credit history at all usually results in a substantial allocation of minus points, perhaps 20 or 30 of them.
- ◆ Having a bank account that's in order: plus 20 points; having

a building society deposit account: plus 10 points.

◆ Having a mortgage with a clean payment record for more than five years: 15 plus points; a mortgage for more than five with one or two delayed payments: plus 10 points; a mortgage for less than five years with a clean payment record: plus 10 points; a mortgage, no matter for how long, with more than three delayed payments: minus 15 points.

◆ The scoring can become very complicated when mainstream credit cards (Barclaycard, Mastercard, American Express, etc.) are being considered. While you generally get plus points (perhaps up to 20 or 30 of them in total) for having up to three credit card accounts in good order, you can actually at times lose points if you have more credit cards than that, especially if you're often operating these quite close to your credit limit.

◆ Store credit cards. Assuming that the accounts are being properly conducted, you may get a few plus points – five or ten of them – for having in-store credit, but if you have a whole bunch of these – say, more than five – you could be penalised with a few minus points because some lenders interpret this as possible evidence of someone who is sailing dangerously close to the wind.

◆ How lenders score accounts that are or have been delinquent varies greatly For example, having just one County Court judgment registered against you may carry a massive penalty of minus points with a lender who only wants Grade A applicants, but may be scored much lower by a lender whose business is aimed at generating high profits by charging very expensive rates of interests to people who have difficulty obtaining credit elsewhere.

Apart from all these variables, there is one more very important factor that will affect any final decision and that's what *kind* of credit you're asking for. While no lender will take on a customer they expect to default, the financial consequences of default to the lender can be mitigated to a great extent if the loan is additionally *secured* in some other way.

❑ The most common form of a secured loan is a mortgage where at the end of the day if the deal goes completely sour, the lender can eventually – after due (and lengthy) court process – repossess the house and sell it to clear all or at least usually most of what's outstanding.

❑ Apart from holding a first mortgage on a property, providing a loan that's also secured on it will provide the next best level of security for a lender – and that's one of the reasons why so many finance companies are eager to lend to any homeowner, no matter how dismal their financial affairs may be.

❑ Hire purchase agreements also provide some additional security for the lender because if things do end belly-up, they can at least repossess the goods and get some money back. The weight lenders give to the security provided by the possibility of repossession varies greatly according to the type of goods bought on HP.

❑ Another way of giving additional security to the lender is for the borrower to get someone to guarantee or co-sign the loan agreement. The value allocated to any guarantee will, of course, depend on the credit worthiness of the guarantor who before entering any such agreement must bear in mind that he or she is completely and totally liable for making good any defaults by the borrower.

HOW TO TURN REFUSAL INTO APPROVAL

Should your application for credit be repeatedly turned down, there are still several things you can do that can cause the decision to be reversed:

First of all, ask the lender why your application was refused, as he will be duty-bound to offer you an explanation, especially if the decision was made on the basis of information received from a third party. Then act as follows:

❑ If you're told that you were turned down because of something on your credit file, find out specifically what this was. Although it is assumed that you've already done everything possible to clean up your credit record (as explained in depth in the previous chapter), you may still be able to take the sting out of one or two bad entries by explaining to the lender why these occurred – and why they won't happen again.

❑ If the reason given for refusal is that you failed to attain the minimum requirement of the lender's credit scoring system, find out – as far as they will tell you – in what areas you got low marks. If there are good reasons why your score is not truly indicative of your creditworthiness, once again offer explanations and assurances, and ask for the decision to be reviewed.

❑ Also ask for the decision to be reconsidered when you're not given any clear-cut reason for refusal.

Difficult though this may be to believe, it still remains a fact that many an application for credit that failed the first time around can still be approved if you persevere. The reasons for this are three-fold:

1. The first decision is usually made by someone at a fairly low level within the lender's organisation and who is only empowered to exactly follow the rules. If your application fails to meet the laid-down criteria, someone in that position has no choice but to say no.

2. All this can change drastically when you ask for a refusal to be reviewed as your application will then be looked at by someone more senior who will invariably have some discretion and doesn't have to be so slavish in interpreting the rules. What this means in practice is that, to carry on with the example directly above, is that he might say, in effect: 'Yes, the application failed to pass the score system. On the other hand, taking everything into consideration, this is still a good bet for us.'

3. In some cases, you may be given credit – both literally and figuratively – for perseverance. Some lenders take the view that if you actively pursue your request despite an initial no, you're showing determination and this in itself can count in your favour, perhaps enough to tip the balance in a borderline case.

CHOOSE A LENDER WHO MATCHES YOUR CIRCUMSTANCES

What type of lender you approach can also make a big difference your chances of success. Here's a brief run-down on the various types of lenders, together with details of some that are particularly worth approaching if your credit record is not all that it could be.

THE HIGH STREET BANKS

Somewhat contrary to what is generally believed, banks can at times be remarkably flexible in how they score credit worthiness, being often prepared to overlook past financial difficulties more readily than many other lenders.

Some useful tips to help you negotiate a loan or other credit facilities with a bank:

- ❑ If you can, open an account with your chosen bank some months before you apply – an existing customer, no matter how recent, is always looked on more favourably.
- ❑ Although you can apply for most kinds of bank credit by post, it is normally best to avoid this method. Instead arrange for an appointment with as senior a member of staff as possible. Postal applications tend to be credit-scored first, and if the result of that is borderline, you're already at a considerable disadvantage. On the other hand, if you first make a favourable impression during a face-to-face meeting and are told that everything looks okay, subject to credit checks, then a minor hiccup later is more likely to be smoothed over.
- ❑ Perhaps more than any other lenders, bank officials will appreciate total candour by applicants. If there are black spots in your credit history, don't seek to hide them, but reveal them frankly. Bankers know that many of their best customers today are people who had problems in the past.

BUILDING SOCIETIES – YOUR NEXT BEST BET

Building societies tend to be less tolerant of chequered credit histories than banks. However, building societies are operating nowadays in a fiercely competitive marketplace and, as a result, have been forced to become a good deal more realistic about what applicants they consider acceptable.

As a result, many building societies are making mortgages more easily available to people who they otherwise might have turned down. Here are three societies that either directly, or through one of their subsidiaries, can be expected to look more favourably on 'problem' applications:

❑ The Britannia Building Society – ask for your application to be considered by its subsidiary, Verso.

❑ The Nationwide – ask for your application to be considered by its subsidiary, UCB Home Loan.

❑ The Woolwich, has been running a scheme called New Start that's aimed specifically at new borrowers with previous payment problems.

To locate your local office of these national institutions, look in your phone book.

As far as which other building societies are likely to be most receptive, it's impossible to list these because the situation is changing almost on a daily basis as societies merge or become banks. However, follow these tips to identify societies that at a given moment are most desperate to lend and will therefore be at their most accommodating:

❑ Look in the newspapers for societies backed are currently under pressure to merge or become banks because these will be trying very hard to have the maximum amount possible out on loan.

❑ Also look for ads from building societies trying to entice borrowers to move from their current one, especially when the ad promises to pay for all the costs of moving the mortgage, offers a low fixed rate for several years, and even throws in a 'cash-back' offer. Such advertising is evidence of a society that *badly* needs new borrowers.

GETTING A CREDIT CARD WHEN OTHERS HAVE REFUSED YOU

Obtaining a credit card can be difficult if your credit history is chequered because these lenders almost invariably base their decisions solely on how well you fare under their scoring system. But there are exceptions to this rule and two credit card providers well known for taking on applicants their opposite numbers might turn down are:

❑ MBNA Europe Bank Ltd. This is the UK arm of a vast American corporation that's slicing itself an ever-increasing portion of the credit card cake by using innovative methods. MBNA takes pride in that they don't use credit-scoring as such but instead rely on what they call 'judgmental lending', a process that looks at three main factors: the applicant's stability, ability to pay, and willingness to pay. That assessment method can come up with quite different answers than those obtained by traditional scoring scheme. What's more, MBNA takes a very enlightened attitude to less than perfect applicants, often preferring to offer them a card with a low limit (as little as £500) rather than turn them down altogether. Find out more by contacting *MBNA Europe Bank Ltd, PO 1004, Chester Business Park, Chester CH4 9WW. Tel: 0800 062 062.*

❑ TSB Card Services. The initials stand for Trustees Savings Bank, and organisation that is now part of Lloyds Bank, but which is said to still retain some of its former more liberal practices, being particularly good at giving credit-seekers the benefit of the doubt if their application only just fails to meet the scoring requirement. Contact them at: *TSB Bank Ltd, Brighton BN1 4BE. Tel: 0845 072 3333.*

FINANCE COMPANIES AND CREDIT BROKERS

It is usually cheaper to borrow from a bank or building society, but finance companies can nevertheless provide a reasonable alternative, especially if the amount of the loan sought is comparatively small and the higher interest charged by these organisations therefore not quite so important.

There are many finance companies that are either known for being prepared to look favourably upon applicants with a defective credit history or who deliberately seek them out by advertising that even someone with one or more County Court judgments, in arrears, or self-employed without proper accounts to prove income is not automatically ruled out. Note, however, that in some instances the names listed below are finance brokers who would not be lending you the money themselves but arrange for a loan on your behalf with a third party lender, a service for which you'd have to pay a fee.

First of all, here are the names and phone numbers of finance organisations, listed in alphabetical order, that offer 'any purpose' loans:

- **Britannia Capital Securities** – 0800 132952.
- **Halifax** – 0845 850 1694.
- **Holmes Court Securities** – 0800 566664.
- **Ironmarket Home Loans and Mortgages Ltd** – 0800 7314744.
- **Lastever Loans** – 0800 929935.
- **LoansUK** – 0800 298 7741.
- **Norton Finance** – 0800 929100.
- **Ocean Finance** – 0800 916 9165.
- **Purple Loans** – 0800 528 3509.

Offering services similar to those listed above, but specialising in mortgages and re-mortgages in which the loan is secured upon the property are:

- **Abbey Finance** – 01733 333847.
- **APS Mortgages** – 0800 043 5678.
- **Bollin Finance Ltd** – 0800 731 4015.
- **CS Company Services Ltd** – 0870 420 4896.
- **Mortgage Company** – 0800 183 0000.
- **The Mortgage Lender** – 0800 316 7123.
- **Weaver Finance Brokers Ltd** – 0800 262 135.

HIRE PURCHASE – A DIFFERENT KIND OF LENDING

Hire purchase differs from any other type of borrowing because the lender can ultimately repossess the goods if you fail to keep up your payments. One other thing that is also different about most hire purchase agreements is that they in fact involve three separate parties: you as the purchaser of the goods who commits himself to pay for them; the lender who puts up the money; and the vendor from whom you buy the goods and who usually gets a commission from the lender for bringing him your business.

As the vendor has a dual interest in seeing the deal go through – not only will he make a sale but will also collect a good chunk of commission on the hire purchase agreement – he can be a powerful ally to have on your side if your application for credit is one that otherwise may be not have been accepted by the lender. Dealers – whether they're selling cars, household goods, or whatever – are the source of a great deal of profitable business for hire purchase companies and, as such, can exert considerable influence on your behalf, enough to at times turn what would been a refusal into an acceptance.

A couple of tips to make sure that dealer from whom you buy is in the best possible position to help your application for credit go through:

❑ If possible and if the price is right, buy from a large organisation – a big business will have more clout to exert on your behalf with the lender than a smaller one.

❑ When dealing with one of the big multiples, buy when they're having a sale. Not only should the price be better, but the manager of the branch will be under even greater pressure to achieve sales targets and therefore will try all the harder to get your deal approved.

HOW MUCH INTEREST WILL YOU PAY?

There is one more important factor that you must consider in all forms of credit: the interest that you will have to pay. By law, lenders have to show interest as an Annual Percentage Rate (APR), a calculation that takes into account both the amount of money outstanding as well as the length of time over which it remains due.

APR is meant to provide a simple yardstick by which borrowers can compare the relative cost of dealing with different lenders. While comparing APRs does work in most cases, be aware that this does not always reveal the whole truth about the cost of a loan because certain charges do not to have to be included in the APR calculation.

Notable exceptions not included in APRs and which can distort the picture are:

❑ Account maintenance and 'activity' charges, such as those levied on some accounts by the high street banks.

❑ Compulsory credit protection insurance premium on a bank overdraft.

❑ Optional credit protection insurance. Be aware that that so-called 'optional' insurance of this type is often sold so subtly that you're not even aware that you've bought it – and, of course, are paying for it on top of the quoted APR.

❑ Equally excluded from the APR is *any* credit insurance protection insurance that includes an element of life cover.

Because of these various permutations, compare the cost of different types of credit not just on their APRs, but also on whether any of the extras charges listed above apply.

ALTERNATIVE WAYS TO BORROW

This chapter has been devoted wholly to what can be called 'mainstream lenders', that is organisations whose business it is to lend money or grant credit facilities, but there are many other ways to borrow or obtain money and these will be examined in the next chapter.

Chapter Five

Alternative Ways To Borrow Money Or Get Credit

When we want to borrow, most of us will usually think in the first instance about approaching the so-called 'mainstream' lenders, such as the big banks, the credit card providers and the numerous other institutions that are household names. Indeed, in many cases, that is perhaps the best avenue to explore first.

However, there are many other potential sources of loans or credit, and in many cases some of these less obvious ones can easily be either more advantageous or more approachable, especially if you've had credit problems in the past.

There now follows brief outlines of these 'alternative' sources, together with handy hints to help you make the most of the opportunities they can offer.

FAMILY AND FRIENDS

Much can be said in favour of borrowing money from people you already know and who therefore also already know you. Obvious candidates as sources of loans, especially if the amounts involved are relatively small and will be repaid over a very short term, are family, friends and other acquaintances. While you may be reluctant to, as it were, 'trade' on a personal relationship to borrow money, there is nothing intrinsically wrong in this as long as both you and the lender are perfectly happy to enter into a suitable arrangement, each of you being totally aware of all aspects involved in the transaction. Do bear in mind, however, that although raising money on the basis of either kinship or friendship can make the whole process much easier, it can also bring its own problems. Here are some important points you should consider before heading down that route:

❑ It's absolutely vital that you should always make a personal lender fully aware of your financial situation, this naturally including all the relevant details about your ability to repay whatever you borrow. Commercial lenders are set up to shrewdly calculate the risk they take whenever they lend money, but personal lenders are entitled to total candour from the borrower.

❑ Naturally, if you were to fail to repay a loan from family members or friends, this will almost certainly lead to a major deterioration in the personal relationship.

❑ Never, but never seek to borrow more from personal contacts than they can reasonably afford to lose.

FINANCIAL HELP FROM EMPLOYERS

Another often overlooked but a perfectly legitimate source of credit is your employer, especially if you need the money for a purpose that is either directly or indirectly linked to your employment.

Most likely to be willing make a loan to an employee are usually the very small businesses – the two- or three-man bands – or the very large ones. The are two good reasons for this:

❑ The smaller the business you work for, the greater will be your proportionate role in it. This means that your employer may well be favourably inclined towards helping you out of a tight spot because he values what you do and doesn't want you unduly worried about your finances.

❑ The really big organisations, like Ford or British Telecom, take employee welfare and morale very seriously and invariably will have a special department in their corporate structure that's charged with providing help, advice, and guidance on any personal problems employees may encounter. Usually, this 'welfare' arm of the business will also have access to a fund from which loans can be made when these can be justified as also being for the direct or indirect benefit of the employer.

It's worth keeping in mind that when seeking to borrow from an employer, you'll always increase your chances of success if you can make a convincing case that the money will be used for something that's linked, even ever so tenuously, to work. For example, an employer is more likely to lend you money to buy a car you need to get to work than to advance cash for a holiday.

HOME CREDIT PROVIDES QUICK
DECISIONS AT A PRICE

A potential source of credit worth considering when the amount required is comparatively small and mainstream institutions have been reluctant to lend because of a chequered credit history is that provided by the 'home credit' industry, this nowadays often referred to as 'weekly collected credit'. These are the relatively new terms used to describe what in bygone years were known as 'tallymen', the seemingly omnipresent doorstep salesmen who provided either cash loans or goods on credit by calling on their customers at their homes and then collecting the instalments during further regular visits.

This is a sector of the credit industry that has experienced some unfortunate image problems in the past, but in certain situations there is still a great deal to be said in favour of this form of borrowing and some of its inherent advantages will become obvious in the following brief description of how it works in practice:

Instead of relying heavily on references or credit scoring systems, home lenders will usually make their decisions on their personal opinion of the borrower, this opinion, of course, usually being based on years of experience together with an intimate knowledge of the local community. This means that in most cases, a decision is usually made immediately. It also means that someone with a chequered credit history who is unable to get a loan from a mainstream lender is much more likely to succeed in getting one from a home lender.

Loans obtained under weekly collected credit schemes are mostly for quite small amounts, perhaps as little as £50 in some cases, but they can also be for much greater sums. Generally, the loans are not intended to finance major capital expenditures but are instead used for comparatively routine expenses, such as car repairs, children's school clothes, the purchase of a washing machine or a holiday. Typically, the loans are repaid on a weekly basis (because most customers are on a weekly income cycle), the instalments collected by the lender's agent. In some instances, the required goods will be supplied directly by the credit provider instead of cash.

Home credit can be a very expensive way of borrowing – typical APRs being much higher than those of other lenders – but these lenders are usually a good deal more flexible and understanding about occasional missed payments than other lenders, accepting these as something that's part and parcel of their particular section of the industry.

To find a home credit lender, look under Credit and Finance Companies in your *Yellow Pages* directory. Alternatively, you can contact the Consumer Credit Association (address in the *Appendix*) for the name of member organisations near where you live.

CREDIT UNIONS – GIVING CREDIT WHERE CREDIT IS DUE

Unlike the prevailing situation in the United States and Australia where credit unions are often multi-million pound businesses, these organisations tend to be much smaller in this country, most often consisting of a small group of volunteers who operate a fund that collects deposits from its members and then makes loans from this central pool.

These unions are generally based on some sort of 'affinity' that links its members in some specific way; for example, membership in a given credit union may be restricted to people who work in a certain place, live in a particular area, or even belong to the same church.

Relatively small though credit unions tend to be, they do offer two very distinct advantages for borrowers:

❑ Their interest rates are very, very low, this being made possible by the fact that credit unions have virtually no overheads.

❑ Decisions about granting loans are usually made quickly, being made by the officers of the organisation, who base their conclusions upon what they know about intending borrowers as individuals, rather than what their credit history may or may not be. There are also two possible disadvantages:

❑ You almost certainly have to be a member in good standing for some time before you can apply for a loan from a credit union. Most commonly, you will have to have been a regular depositor for some months before you can borrow.

❑ How much you can borrow will usually be limited to a fairly small amount, perhaps as little as £1,000, and often even much less than that.

If credit unions sound like the answer to your problems, you can locate one near you by either getting in touch with your local Citizens' Advice Bureau or writing to the two following national organisations:

1) *The National Federation of Savings and Co-operative Credit Unions*, 39 Cavendish Avenue, New Malden, Surrey KT3 QH; or

2) *The Association of British Credit Unions Ltd*, Hollyoake House, Hanover Street, Manchester M60 0AS.

A DIFFERENT WAY OF BORROWING

There is yet one more very useful way to borrow money that can under some circumstances offer the very best of all deals. That method is pawnbroking, the system that basically consists of you putting up something of value as security for the money you borrow.

To borrow money against the security of a pledge is probably the oldest type of credit transaction and the origins of pawnbroking can be traced back more than 3,000 years to the Chinese, who appear to have invented it.

Put at its very simplest, a pawnbroker makes his living on the interest he charges on a loan made against a pledged item. Here is how it works:

❑ To begin with, the pawnbroker estimates the value of the goods being offered as pledges before entering into a loan agreement. Be aware beforehand that a pawnbroker's valuation of a pledge may be a lot less than what you might expect. For example, a stereo set that sells new for £500 may be valued as low as £50 as a pledge.

❑ When an item is accepted as a pledge for a loan, the customer is given a credit agreement that also is the pawn receipt. By law, certain information must be listed on this document, including:

1) the names and addresses of both parties,

2) a schedule of the property pledged,

3) full details of the *total amount payable* under the agreement for a full period of six months, this sum broken down into its separate components, such as any charge payable on issue of the document, and how much it will cost to redeem the pledged item/s.

❑ You don't have to wait until the end of the agreement to get your property back, but can redeem it any time beforehand by paying what is owed under the agreement.

❑ Should it be impossible for you to reclaim the goods you have pledged by the deadline specified in the agreement, the pawnbroker *may* agree to extend your loan, so effectively giving you more time to come up with the money.

❑ However, if the agreement is not extended, what happens if you haven't redeemed your goods by paying all that's outstanding under the agreement by the end of the period of the loan, depends upon how much you borrowed in the first place:

A) If the loan was for £75 or a smaller amount, the pawned property becomes the property of the pawnbroker.

B) If the loan was for more than £100, the pawnbroker can proceed to sell the pledge/s to get his money back. In that case, he will have to give you at least 14 days' written notice of his intention to sell and this notice must state what the asking price for the item/s will be as well as give details of when, how, and where they are to be sold. You retain the right to redeem your pledges until they're actually sold.

C) If the original loan was for more than £75 but no more than £100, the pawnbroker can sell the pledge/s without first having to inform you.

❑ If the pledge is sold, the pawnbroker must send you a notice within 20 working days of the sale that tells you how much the sale realised and what the costs were of making the sale. When selling the goods, the pawnbroker is obliged to do his best to obtain their true market value on the date of the sale because if the sale realises a surplus beyond what he is owed (this being the loan and accrued interest and charges), that surplus belongs to you. On the other hand, if the pledge/s sell for less than what you owe, you remain liable for the difference. Note, however, that when there is a surplus, the pawnbroker does not *have* to send this amount to you unless you claim it; so if you get a notice saying that your pawn sold for more than what was owed, write back immediately and ask that the difference be sent to you without delay.

Like every other form of borrowing, using a pawnbroker has distinct advantages and disadvantages. These can be summed up as follows:

The good points:

❑ It's a very convenient way to raise money quickly.

❑ The goods you pledge remain your property during the length of the agreement and you can be sure of getting them back if you meet the agreed payments.

The bad points:

❑ The interest charged by pawnbrokers is usually quite high.

❑ If you eventually find that you are unable to redeem your pledge and it ends up being sold by the pawnbroker, you may be more than just a little disappointed by how low a price it fetches.

LENDERS OF FINAL RESORT

The various types of lenders mentioned so far will, of course, be trading legally and will therefore also operate in accordance with the various codes of conducts or other guidelines that may have been formulated by their respective trade associations.

But there are also illegal lenders, whose operations are completely outside the law. More commonly known as 'loan sharks', these lenders, ranging from individuals to sizeable gangs, are extremely bad news for any borrower who has the misfortune to deal with them. Here are some of the reasons why that is so:

❑ The interest charged is always staggeringly high – typically, it will cost £6 to repay £5 borrowed only for a week, that is the equivalent of 20% *a week*, or an APR of more than 1,000%!

❑ Because loan sharks operate outside the law, they cannot take a delinquent debtor to court and therefore frequently resort to intimation, harassment and even physical violence to enforce payment.

❑ Loan sharks are also notorious for the various nefarious means they employ to ensure that a borrower remains in their clutches, such as forcing him to take out additional loans to 'repay' an original one so that the debt becomes a self-perpetuating vicious circle of misery in which ever-increasing extortionate interest keeps getting piled on.

While it is understandable that someone generally desperate for a loan and unable to get it through other means may consider using an illegal lender, there still remains only one piece of advice that can be offered: *Don't do it!*

LOANS FROM YOUR FRIENDLY GOVERNMENT

One more possible source of loans for people who may have difficulty raising money elsewhere is the Social Fund, which is operated by the Benefits Agency, an agency of the Government's Department of Works and Pensions.

All too often ignored as a possible source of cash, the Social Fund can lend money in a wide variety of circumstances. Essentially, it makes two kinds of loans – so-called Budgeting Loans or Crisis Loans. The rules for getting these vary according to the type of loan. These are the key points:

❑ Budgeting Loans are free of interest of any kind and are intended to make it possible for people on limited incomes to buy items that they would otherwise find it difficult to save or budget for, but you may also be able to get a loan to help with existing hire purchase commitments and some other debts. Says the Benefits Agency: 'Each application is judged on its own merits.'

❑ To qualify for a Budgeting Loan you must have been receiving Income Support or income-based Jobseeker's Allowance, or have been the partner of someone receiving these benefits, for at least 26 weeks, although a minor gap in this period can be ignored.

❑ The amount you may be allowed to borrow will depend on the cost of the item you intend to buy, and whether the Social Fund Officer considers that expense a reasonable one, as well as your ability to repay. The maximum amount that you can borrow is £1,000; the minimum, £30.

❑ The rate of repayment is variable and will take into account any other commitments you already have, but generally the loan will have to be paid back at a rate between 5p and 15p for every £1 of Income Support you get over a period of 18 months.

❑ Equally interest-free are Crisis Loans, which, as the name indicates, are meant to meet urgent needs in an emergency. Apart from the fact that you have to be aged 16 years or over, there are no other set qualifications.

❑ Typical examples of Crisis Loans are advances to people who lost their money, lost things in a fire or are stranded away from home. These, however, are only examples, and you can still apply if your circumstances are different from those described above.

To apply for a Social Fund loan, contact your nearest Benefits Agency office – you'll find its address listed in your local phone book.

Appendix

Where To Get Additional Help And Advice

Apart from the various official bodies and other organisations already mentioned elsewhere, there are many others who can offer most useful help and advice, this generally being totally free for the asking.

Call Credit,
    Consumer Services Team,
    PO Box 491,
    Leeds LS3 1WZ,
    Tel: 0870 060 1414;
    website: www.callcredit.plc.uk.

Citizens' Advice Bureaux, National Association,
    Myddelton House,
    115-123 Pentonville Road,
    London N1 9LZ
    website: www.citizensadvice.org.uk

This national organisation has more than 700 local offices and you'll find at least one in every major town or city. Citizens' Advice Bureaux – or CABs, as they're generally known, will provide free completely independent and impartial advice on a wide range of subjects, these specifically including credit and debt problems.

As well as being invaluable sources of information, CABs can also often give practical help – such as for instance, aiding with filling in forms or drafting letters for people who might have some difficulties doing this themselves. To find your nearest CAB, look in your local phone book, ask your local council, or phone the number listed above.

Council of Mortgage Lenders (CML),
3 Saville Row,
London W1S 3PB.
Tel: 020-7437 0075.

All mortgage lending institutions are eligible for membership of this organisation which was established in 1989 as a central body for the various businesses that together constitute the housing finance industry. It publishes *The Mortgage Code*, which sets out standards for lenders, runs the Council of Mortgage Lenders' Arbitration Scheme, and also operates the CML Possessions Register, details of which are held on file by the credit reference agencies.

Credit Industry Fraud Avoidance System (CIFAS),
173-175 Cleveland Street,
London W1P 5PE.

A non-profit making organisation whose membership includes all major credit grantors, CIFAS provides a framework, through the credit reference agencies, for the exchange of information about fraudulent attempts to obtain credit.

Data Protection Registrar, The,
Wycliffe House,
Water Lane,
Wilmslow,
Cheshire, SK9 5AF.

Equifax Europe (UK) Ltd,
Credit File Advice Centre,
PO Box 1140,
Bradford BD1 5US;
Tel: 0870 010 0583;
website: www.equifax.co.uk.

Experian Ltd,
Consumer Help Service,
PO Box 8000,
Nottingham NG1 5GX;
Tel: 0870 241 6212;
website: www.Experian.co.uk.

Information Commissioner, The,
Wycliffe House,
Wilmslow,
Cheshire SK9 5AF;
Tel:(01625) 545 745;
website: www.dataprotection.gov.uk.

Office of Fair Trading (OFT),
Field House,
15-25 Bream's Building,
London EC4A 1PR.

This is a government department that is charged with a wide range of duties concerned with protecting consumers and encouraging competition. The OFT publishes a number of free information booklets that can be obtained either from them or also usually from your local Trading Standards office. Particularly worth looking at are *CreditWise: your guide to trouble-free credit; Your Mortgage: a guide to repayment methods;* and *Debt: what to do when bills pile up.* You can call the OFT Consumer Information Line – Tel: 0345 224 499 (calls charged at local rate) – for free guidance on where practical help can be obtained if problems arise in the purchase of goods and services.

Registry Trust Limited,
173-175 Cleveland Street,
London, W1P 5PE.

This is the organisation that maintains the official Register of County Court Judgments.

Trading Standards Departments

These are offices run by your local authority that can provide free information and advice on a wide range of consumer problems. You'll find the address of your nearest one in your local telephone book under your county, regional or borough council. In Northern Ireland, contact *The Department of Economic Development, Trading Standards Branch, 176 Newtonbreda Road, Belfast BT8 4QS.*

Other Books from Windsor

egar, Nature's Secret
eapon – Our No.1 bestseller.
e vinegar for health and around
 house PLUS Honey and Garlic
us sections.

ean Your Liver – Help your
dy's 'detox machine' improve
r health.

e Diabetics Guide to
althy Living – Improve blood
gar levels, boost energy, feel
0% better.

w to Relieve the Pain of
thritis – The latest break-
oughs and information all suf-
ers should have!

block Your Arteries
How to beat Britian's No.1 killer.

e Sciatica Relief
ndbook – natural ways to
vent flare-ups.

opping Restless Legs
ndrome – millions sleep
sy again with these natural
edies.

Alternative IBS Treatments
– practical solutions for IBS problems.

The Complete Guide to Tinnitus and Deafness
– tried and tested remedies for lasting relief.

Improve Your Eyesight
– exercise, diet and great tips to improve your eyesight.

Relief from Psoriasis
– get relief for psoriasis and prevent further flare-ups.

Fibromyalgia Relief Handbook – Don't suffer in silence. Get all the facts and latest treatments.

The Gout Relief Handbook
– find out which foods help keep gout away. Plus all the latest treatments.

Back Pain? How to Stop it
– beat back pain with the latest methods.

The Potent Man – improve virility and regain your libido.

Foot Infections Handbook
– keep troublesome foot and nail complaints at bay.

The Rosacea Handbook
– new remedies and how and why they work.

Grow New Hair – Contrary to popular belief, balding and hair loss can be reversed.

Hydrogen Peroxide: for your Health and for your Home – astonishing uses around the home – and for your health.

Prostate Problems
– essential reading for every man aged 45+.

Garden Magic – hundreds of tips for a beautiful garden.

Free for Seniors – get your share of the millions on offer from the government.

Government Cash Benefits Handbook – find out how much money the government owes you.

Fly Anywhere in the World

Absolutely FREE

(Or For Next to Nothing)

An Introduction To Air Courier Travel

Introduction To Air Courier Travel

Air courier travel represents perhaps the very best way to travel free or at a ludicrously low cost to yourself.

Generally, courier firms deal in time sensitive material. They need some means of transporting products, documents and packages to all parts of the world, without having to put their trust in the postal services, or other delivery firms. But, it is not just a question of making sure these items actually reach their intended destination. They usually have to do so in as short a space of time as possible. Very few high-speed delivery firms have sufficient workload to warrant employing full-time staff to carry articles abroad. Hence the need for freelance operators to act as regular or standby couriers.

Items you might be asked to accompany abroad include: letters, photographs, legal papers, contracts, business proposals, computer disks, reports, product prototypes, and so on. At other times you might be asked to accompany urgent deliveries, such as medicines left behind by travellers. Or deliver foreign delicacies for smart international restaurants, and so on. Several firms specialise in speedy transportation of sensitive material, each of them vying for honour as speediest service available.

The main reason firms use couriers depends on whether packages are classed as baggage or cargo. Cargo needs no courier and will take two day or more to reach its destination. Personal baggage - items which are accompanied by a courier - can reach their destination in just a few hours.

Couriers are rarely needed to physically collect or deliver packages. Company representatives at points of departure and arrival normally handle all packages. You simply obtain clearance through Customs for whatever you accompany. After that, you are free to go your own way. Perhaps enjoy a long vacation in whatever country you find yourself. It couldn't be easier!

Anyone over 18, in good health, can become a courier. Nationality is usually unimportant, and one does not need to be of the same nationality as the airline used. Retired people are more than welcome to operate as couriers with most firms.

Getting Started

Applying for a flight couldn't be easier. All you do is call any of the courier firms listed in the directory which follows a little later on, or, alternatively, approach international high-speed delivery firms listed in Yellow Pages. Tell them you'd like to operate as a courier, and if necessary, make known your preferences for destination and timing. If you can leave the destination open, you stand a very good chance of regular free trips. The firm will keep your information on file and will inform you of openings, sometimes without notice, and what fare (if any) you will have to pay.

Some firms give applicants a list of destinations, prices, schedules and likely future requirements, maybe requiring them to sign and return a contract outlining their responsibilities and duties while acting on behalf of the courier firm.

When you are offered a flight, you will usually be asked to telephone the company as the flight date draws near, just to make sure you are honouring your obligations.

Your ticket will be waiting for you at the airport. Normally, you will be handed just the outward ticket, until your role is fulfilled. Representatives of the courier firm will meet you at the airport of arrival, where you will have to wait a short time, while items you have accompanied are processed through Customs.

Exactly when you can travel can have a significant effect on the price you pay for your seat. You will almost certainly pay a far higher price where your booking is made well in advance of the flight, than will be so for last minute or emergency flights.

If you can travel at short - or no notice, do so. You'll probably travel free. A flight that might cost £150 if booked well in advance, will usually be offered at something nearer £15 - sometimes free - to a standby courier.

Destinations

You will only be able to visit areas serviced by the courier firm you operate with. Some fly to just one destination, others to several; many cover most major international towns and cities. If you restrict yourself to one courier firm, you will obviously limit the number of places you might visit. So make yourself known to several courier firms, in particular those operating on an international basis.

Until recently, all couriers travelled free. Today, although there are still many opportunities for free travel, most firms set a small charge.

Just how long you will be allowed to remain abroad, is a matter for mutual agreement between yourself and the courier firm. Dates of departure and return are agreed prior to the flight, and form part of your contract with the company. Only in the most exceptional circumstances might an extension to your original stay abroad be considered. In emergency or unforeseen circumstances, the courier company will almost certainly be sympathetic to your request, however might nevertheless, make a small charge for rescheduling your return flight.

Your contract will normally provide for a charge to be levied against you in the event of you cancelling your flight. The actual amount will depend on the amount of notice you give the company. If you cancel at the last moment, you will probably forfeit your payment.

Travel Insurance

All travellers abroad should take out insurance against loss and damage to possessions, and for illness and injury to themselves.

Sometimes you will be offered insurance by the courier company, sometimes not. Make sure you are covered. It is a very inexpensive option indeed, and can save a great deal of heartache and money.

Courier companies usually provide cover at very competitive rates. Alternatively, cover can be arranged through brokers over the telephone with payment by credit card. Some supermarkets offer this type of insurance as well as travel agents, the AA, Thomas Cook etc. Also, visit website addresses for competitive quotes, such as:

www.a-z-insurance.co.uk/travel
www.cheapest-travel-insurance.co.uk
www.underthesun.co.uk
www.norwich-union.co.uk/products/insurance/travel

Some companies allow anyone over 18 years, and in reasonably good health, to fly with them. Some do not employ couriers over 65. Check this at the outset.

What problems and inconveniences you might encounter are very few and relatively minor. Perhaps the biggest is the fact that sometimes you will be restricted to hand luggage only. Since the courier company's packages are effectively using what would otherwise be your space as passenger.

A hold-all or sports bag should carry sufficient clothing and personal items to provide for most short stays. Remember also, that most airlines distinguish between duty frees and hand luggage. You should therefore be able to take both on board with you. Not a bad return for even the shortest of stays abroad!

What other potential problems might confront the courier? Imprisonment - or worse - for carrying illegal drugs, might be the first problem that springs to mind for the more sceptical reader. Fortunately, very few problems exist here, since established courier companies have a reputation to uphold, and screening of packages is an essential feature of pre-flight arrangements.

Furthermore, all airlines carry out extensive checks of packages for drugs, weapons, bombs, and any other of life's more unfortunate paraphernalia. If this isn't sufficient to allay your fears, then remember that you have a contact stating that you are just a courier.

Warning

Stick to well-known, established courier firms! Do not carry items abroad for anyone else!

When your flight day arrives, you will be told where to meet the courier firm's representatives. More often than not, it will be the departure airport terminal, an hour or two before the flight.

Usually, a company representative will meet you, and book you onto the plane. Documents, and other smaller packages might be handed to you to carry during the flight. You will also be fully briefed on what is expected of you during, and shortly after, the flight. Most companies also expect you to dress smartly during the flight. You are representing them, after all!

Tips For Prospective Couriers

First and foremost, you can make yourself virtually indispensable to courier firms, simply by providing first class service; honouring your obligations; looking smart and tidy; being available for virtually all destinations and willing to fly at any time and at very short - or without - notice.

Make yourself available to as many courier firms as possible, particularly any based close to your own local airports. That way, you'll receive priority over couriers from other parts of the country. Try not to give the impression that the low cost - or free - air ticket is your sole interest - even if it is!

Below you will find a list of fairly standard questions asked by potential air couriers together with answers.

Q: Are there any special qualifications required to fly as a courier?

A: Being in possession of a valid passport, and visa to the country you are flying to, if one is required. You must be over 18.

Q: In general, are courier flights one way or return flights?

A: On the whole, courier flights from London are return, but sometimes you can book a one-way flight at about 60% of the regular courier return fare.

Q: How long can I stay at the appointed destination?

A: This varies with the courier company you are working for, and the destination. Some only give a seven day return ticket, while others give an open return ticket for up to one year. In other cases, you can negotiate your return date.

Q: Is it possible to fly from other UK airports apart from London

A: Currently, London is the only 'Courier Gateway' city in the UK.

Q: How much personal luggage can I take with me?

A: Most companies in the UK allow you to take one 20kg bag, as well as a carrying holdall.

Q: How much should I expect to pay for my flight ticket?

A: Rates very much depend on the time of year, destination, and whether the flight has been booked in advance, or at the last minute.

Q: What about my expenses while abroad as a courier?

A: The answer is that you are responsible for your own expenses apart from flights to Australia where there is an overnight stay, if the route is via Tokyo or Bangkok.

Q: What areas of the world are covered from London?

A: Europe, The United States, Africa, South America, Australia and South East Asia.

Courier Companies

(This list was accurate at the time of printing. For further contacts, look in the Yellow Pages under 'Courier Companies', especially for firms based close to international airports.)

Bridges Worldwide
Tel: 01895 465465
Building 521, London Heathrow Airport, Hounslow, Middlesex, TW6 3UJ
Services are to various locations in the US, Tokyo and Bangkok. Most routes are with Virgin Airlines.

Nomad Courier Travel
Tel: 020 8755 1323
664 Hansworth Road, Hounslow, Middlesex, TW4 5NP
Flights to New York.

World Courier Centre UK Ltd.,
Tel: 01753 726999
Express Cargo Terminal, S126, Heathrow, Hounslow, Middlesex, TW6 2JS

Sources Of Further Information

www.britishservices.co.uk/courier.htm
www.aircourier.co.uk